Abc

Christopher Tobin is a journalist and has been the editor of several newspapers. He is presently editor of the *Oamaru Mail*. His interest in the Anzacs grew after learning three great uncles served together in the Canterbury Infantry Battalion at Gallipoli. One of them, a 20-year-old carpenter in civilian life, was killed in action at Rhododendron Spur near Chunuk Bair on August 7, 1915. His previous books include *The Original All Blacks* (2005), *Gone to Gallipoli: Anzacs of small town NZ go to war* (2001) and *Fitzsimmons: Boxing's first triple world champion* (2000).

A New Zealand officer remembers

# April 25, 1915

'The most glorious day of my life'

## Lieutenant Spencer Westmacott

Edited by Christopher P. Tobin

Bosco Press

Lieutenant Spencer Westmacott

First published 2014

Published by Bosco Press
28A Reed St, Oamaru 9400

A catalogue record for this book is available from
the National Library of New Zealand

ISBN 978-0-473-30033-3

Cover image: New Zealand and Australian soldiers landing at Anzac Cove,
Gallipoli, Turkey. New Zealand Free Lance: Photographic prints and negatives.
Ref: PAColl-5936-18. Alexander Turnbull Library, Wellington
Design by IslandBridge
Printed by Otago Daily Times Print, Alexandra, New Zealand

# Contents

# Foreword

This book aims to show New Zealand's path to war in 1914 and the New Zealanders' role in the famous Anzac landing at Gallipoli on April 25, 1915, through the eyes of one who was there, Lieutenant Spencer Westmacott of the Auckland Infantry Battalion's 16th Waikato Company.

Westmacott's account of that day has been described by Major General Sir Howard Kippenberger, a famous New Zealand soldier and a man widely read in military history, as being one of the best and truest testimonies of personal experience in battle that he had ever read.[1]

For this reason alone it is worth reading.

However, the curious thing about April 25, 1915, the day so famously identified as the time New Zealand and Australia took a giant step towards nationhood separate from Britain, is that in military terms it was a failure. The amateur Anzac soldiers showed courage and dash doing their utmost to live up to the Australians' proud boast that they would be in Constantinople "before the pubs close." In doing so, they won the respect of the British generals who had been concerned that the untried "citizen soldiers" from the dominions might not be

---

1 Kippenberger letter to Westmacott dated April 17, 1957, in Westmacott's memoirs, Alexander Turnbull Library, Wellington. Major General Sir Howard Kippenberger served in both world wars and was commander of the 2nd NZ Division during the Italian campaign. He was Editor-in-Chief of *The Official History of NZ in the Second World War 1939–45.* He died May 5, 1957, less than a month after writing to Westmacott.

battle-ready after only six months training. However, in spite of their tremendous courage they never got close to Constantinople, nor did they achieve their chief objective in taking a hill designated as Hill 971. At times, they showed their inexperience and the day could easily have turned to disaster, while the hastily prepared plans by the British commanders proved inept.

Yet because of their courage and daring, the British press lionised the Anzacs, praising them to the heights. It helped create the Anzac legend and later also served the purpose of appeasing feelings of guilt. When Spencer Westmacott reached England as the campaign still raged, he found his relations felt badly about Gallipoli. They believed the New Zealanders and Australians had been tossed into a campaign that was an enormous gamble and doomed from the outset.

On April 25, 1915, Spencer Westmacott was seriously wounded; his platoon was shot to shreds; his friends were killed. But he called this day of failure, this day in which he was maimed for life and nearly died, "the most glorious day of my life." It says a lot about the type of man he was.

*Christopher Tobin*

# Path to war

Spencer Westmacott, or to give his full name, Herbert Horatio Spencer Westmacott, was born in Christchurch, New Zealand, on November 10, 1885. He was called Spencer or Spen for short, and later, in his army years, Westy. His father, Herbert Westmacott, had come to the country from England over 20 years before to prospect for gold in Central Otago.

During a return trip to England, Herbert met a young woman, Ada Janet Depree whom he married. They sailed for New Zealand and settled in Christchurch. By the time Spencer came into the world Herbert was supporting the family by selling horses to the British Army in India.

He would buy four to six-year-old thoroughbreds in Canterbury for 10 to 12 pounds each, and then ship them to India where they would fetch 60 pounds apiece as officers' chargers. Every year Herbert took 100 horses to India which saw him away for up to eight months at a time.

With plenty of horse talk around the family table Spencer became knowledgeable on the subject from a young age and by eight, at a glance, could pick a charger, a Royal Horse Artillery leader, a gun wheeler or an ordinary remount.

Years later he wrote that as a child he was excitable, imaginative and easily roused, qualities suggesting an artistic temperament. Art ran in the family. There had been three generations of famous sculptors of whom the most eminent was his great grandfather, Sir

Richard Westmacott, whose statue "Achilles" in London's Park Lane had been the first public nude statue erected in England. The statue had been commissioned in 1822 by the women of England for Arthur, Duke of Wellington, and his brave companions.

Not surprisingly, Spencer showed an early talent in painting and drawing and also from a young age he became fascinated with the military, partly again because of family associations. A brother of his father, Dick Westmacott, was a general in the British Army in India, and another uncle, Ruscomb, was a colonel in the Lancashire Fusiliers. Spencer corresponded with his Uncle Dick and in Christchurch this fascination saw him go out of his way to talk to war veterans.

One of these was a former Royal Horse Artilleryman, Sergeant Taylor, a veteran of the Indian Mutiny. Taylor worked as a commissionaire outside the DIC department store in central Christchurch and told young Spencer stories of guns being rushed forward to battle. Spencer chatted also with a group of veterans who often sat along a wall in a corner of Christchurch's Cathedral Square from where they watched the world go by. Spencer vowed that when he grew up he would become a soldier like them. Not even the grizzly sight of one veteran who had been horribly wounded and lost his nose in battle deterred him.

In 1896 Spencer started at Christchurch Boys' High School. Here, his military interest was sustained by serving in the cadets. He became friends with two rebellious brothers, Gordon and Robin Harper, both of whom would be awarded the Distinguished Conduct Medal at Gallipoli. With the Harpers, Spencer got up to all sorts of pranks. Detentions failed to stop them and each Monday they were routinely caned. To soften the effects of these Monday morning caning sessions, they would come prepared. Under the seat of his trousers Gordon Harper would wear a dried cat skin while Spencer bolstered his support in the target area by wearing a pair of horse-riding corduroy breeches, hidden, of course, under his usual trousers.

Spencer did not see out his school years at Christchurch Boys'. The desire of his parents was to own a farm and to their delight this came about when they were successful in gaining a ballot for land in the subdivision of Waikahahi, an estate located on highly fertile soil between the Waihoa and Waitaki rivers in South Canterbury.

This followed action by the Liberal Government which had forced the Scottish born owner Allan McLean to sell his estate to the Crown for 323,090 pounds as part of a policy of breaking up largely privately owned properties to create smaller farms.

"My parents rejoiced," Spencer remembered. "The good fortune of drawing a sheep run at the ballot seemed like a direct answer to my father's prayer to Heaven."

While his parents and sister, Erica, settled into Waikakahi, Spencer went to spend a year in Taranaki staying with an uncle, Ned Westmacott. He attended Fitzroy School where he found among his fellow pupils the children of Major Tuke, an officer in charge of imperial troops who had been ordered to take Parihaka and bring out Maori leader Te Whiti in 1881. Parihaka was a small Maori community in Taranaki which had become a centre of a non-violent campaign against European occupation of confiscated land. Spencer relished the military history of the area.

At the end of the year, 1899, he re-joined his family and the next month went to board at Waitaki Boys' High School in the nearby small farm servicing town of Oamaru, North Otago, where he became a bugler in the military cadets.

Again he sought out war veterans. A swagger, Peg-legged Charlie, recounted to him how he lost a leg in the Franco Prussian War in 1870 when serving with the French Army and Spencer came across a former sergeant major named Kibblewhite living in a tent opposite Redcastle, a mansion owned by McLean, the original owner of Waikakahi. Kibblewhite had served with Gustavus von Tempsky's Forest Rangers in the Maori Land Wars during the 1860s. Spencer:

> He had been at Orakau and in all the fighting till his leader fell. He always spoke of him as 'Von' with great affection. He had squandered his pay and also the money he derived from the sale of the land granted him after

the war. It had gone quickly and he spoke with a note of contempt at his folly of wasting it on women.

He liked talking to us boys who could imagine the thrill as the firing commenced and the bullets started to fly. It was all before us, we hoped.

The action at Orakau in 1864 was well known around the country. Kibblewhite would have been part of a British force of 1474 men which attacked the Kingite Maori village of Orakau near Te Awamutu. The Maori led by Rewi Maniapoto had 150 of 300 men and women killed or wounded. The British had 15 killed and 54 wounded.

Spencer and his mates found another veteran, a former Taranaki militia man, living in a two-roomed shack along the Oamaru beach. An Irishman, he described to them being present at the attack on Captain Lloyd's party at Ahuahu in April 1864. This too was an action well known around New Zealand. The Irishman would have been in the 57th Regiment of a newly formed Taranaki Militia when they came under attack from Maori followers of prophet Te Ahuahu. They were on their way to destroy Maori crops and had been resting. Lloyd and six others were killed and decapitated. The others, the Irishman among them, escaped into the bush.

Spencer and his fellow school cadets were also among vast crowds that waved and cheered contingents leaving for the Anglo-Boer War in South Africa, both in Oamaru and Dunedin.

After the 1903 school year, by which time he was a gangling youth standing 6ft 2in tall, he left to join his father on the farm at Waikakahi.

He knew little of farming but under his father's instruction learned quickly. In his spare time he served in the Studholme Mounted Rifles, attended dances and the hunt club ball, or rode into the township of Waimate to a boxing night at the theatre and any show that might be on. His holidays were mounted rifles camps where he came in contact with recently returned troopers from the Anglo-Boer War, many of them hard bitten and hard drinking station hands. Also he made an annual trip to the Grand National steeplechase in Christchurch which was a popular meeting for country people before lambing started. Spencer recalled of his visits to Christchurch:

> Warners bar with two bright barmaids Gertie and Kebie behind the bar; that was the place! It was bright and warm, the lights glowed. All the sporting figures of Canterbury seemed to be there lining the high counter, feet on rail, clustered in front of the fire. There was no measuring the whiskey then. Help yourself. If one seemed to lag, one of the girls would say 'Have one with me' and so it went on.

One year he had a trip to Australia. Then In 1910 with his father's backing, attracted by the prospect of cheap land, he ventured to the North Island and took out a lease on a block east of Te Kuiti and Otorohanga. Shifting to this part of the country was like moving to a different world although friends from Canterbury did the same.

> The South Island of my boyhood might just have well been England, for all that I could learn there of conditions in the King Country bush.

He hired bushmen to clear trees and undergrowth and assisted in the hard physical work. And of course he joined the local territorials.

As Spencer worked to build his life as a farmer much was happening beyond New Zealand. The Western world looked set on a course of war. In 1908 a major conflict had been narrowly averted in Europe after Austria-Hungary had annexed Bosnia and Herzegovina from the Ottoman Empire.

Serbia had mobilised with Russian support. Germany, Austro-Hungary's ally since 1879, then threatened war but eventually the Serbians and Russians, who also had an alliance with France, backed down.

Britain, meanwhile, was in an Entente Cordiale with France and Russia and fearful of Germany which was growing in power. Many in Europe believed Germany was devising a strategy to take on Britain and gain global power. German confidence had grown in step with a boom in their industry.

The situation had arisen that instead of preventing war, alliances between the various nations were heightening tensions and creating a climate which gave the impression Europe could explode at any moment — and New Zealand, as a loyal son of Britain, would be roped into it as well.

A year after Europe went to the brink New Zealand created a compulsory territorial force comprising senior cadets aged from 14 and territorials, 18 to 21, later 25, who could volunteer for overseas service. A colonel on the British General Staff of the 2nd British Division, Alexander Godley, was sent out from England, promoted to major general and put in charge. A former Dublin Fusilier, aged in his 40s and a towering figure standing well over six feet tall, Godley had served in the Anglo-Boer War. He acquired a reputation for aloofness.

Aloof or not, he seemed efficient. Soon he had more than 29,000 territorials and 26,446 senior cadets drilling all around the country, which, given that the total population was less than one million was an achievement.

The British Empire's leading military figure, Field Marshal Lord Kitchener, came to cast his eye over the forces as did the Inspector General of British Overseas Forces, Sir Ian Hamilton, in May 1914, and the country solemnly pledged a mammoth one million pounds to Britain for a new dreadnought battleship, *New Zealand*, that would take 20 years to pay off.

The rise of such strident militarism was opposed vigorously by a newly emerging Labour Party as well as by the New Zealand Peace Council, the Anti-Militaristic League and the Passive Register's Union. Hundreds of young men refused to become part-time soldiers but still, most, and Spencer and his family were among these, considered it their duty to support the government and British Empire militarism.

They talked affectionately of Britain as 'home' and 'the Mother Country'.[1] Certainly Britain was playing its part. From 1911 to 1914

1 In 1914 one in five New Zealand residents had been born in Britain.

it was the destination for 79 percent of New Zealand's exports, especially dairy produce and meat. With this economic lifeline New Zealand was willing to pay back militarily as the country had during the 1899–1902 Anglo-Boer War. The human cost of that conflict had not been too severe. New Zealand sent 6141 troopers of whom, in just over three years, 71 were killed, 25 died in accidents and 133 succumbed to disease.

But to return to Spencer: In the King Country, his lifestyle was similar to what it had been in South Canterbury, revolving around farming and the territorials. In 1911 he gained a commission as second lieutenant in the 16th Waikato Infantry Regiment and for his social life, made occasional trips up to Auckland. One such trip was in May 1913 to see the new one million pound dreadnought *HMS New Zealand* on which a cousin of his, Rupert Westmacott, was serving as a junior officer. Rupert was one of 13 children of Anglican Canon Walter and Maud Westmacott, of Cornwall.

Spencer stayed at the Grand Hotel which was packed with politicians and dignitaries. In spite of being short of money, through his father and family name he had an entry into Auckland society. He attended dances, a ball and had meals with the elite of the city and he and Rupert became close to two sisters, Mary and Esther Foster.

On returning to the King Country, Spencer continued to correspond with Mary and, probably partly as a way to see her again, he returned to Auckland taking a party of territorials and cadets up to view *HMS New Zealand*.

While in Auckland this time Rupert suggested Spencer sail as a guest of the dreadnought to Suva. Spencer was keen on the idea and after seeking out the captain, Captain Halsey, gained his approval.

He was in awe of Captain Halsey. "I was voiceless in his presence and never got to know him." However, he found another officer, Commander Grace, a son of the famous cricketer W.G.Grace, "a genial, kindly man."

At Suva, no ship was available to take him back to New Zealand and so he continued on to Honolulu where, having run out of money, he had to ask Rupert for 20 pounds to pay for his return fare.

Back in the King Country, his adventurous life took another turn in late October 1913 when port workers around the country went on strike. Prime Minister William Massey called for special constable volunteers to keep the ports open and to crush the growing power of the trade union movement. The mayor of Te Kuiti took the names of men, mostly in the mounted rifle territorials, to go to Auckland to help.

Spencer volunteered at once and entrained with 25 others for Auckland. He did not pass on details to his family about his time with 'Massey's Cossacks,' as they were called — a derogatory term — and all he told them was that he rode down Auckland's Queen Street. The strike created bitter divisions between the urban and rural communities. City workers hated Massey for his actions while most of those living in rural areas applauded what they called his decisive action. The reference to calling them 'Massey's Cossacks' came from eight years before when a charge by Cossacks protecting the Czar's Winter Palace against a crowd of 100,000 at St Petersburg left more than 3000 dead.

During the strike, Spencer had more than a few of what he called "trying moments." On one occasion he and his troop escorted horse drawn lorries from Bucklands store off Karangahape Road to the wharf for loading, jeered by crowds all the way. To make matters worse the streets were slippery from overnight rain and in Queen Street, one of the lorry horses fell.

The crowd howling like wolves swayed towards us. A uniformed constable spurred his horse to meet them and his animal came down. Again the crowd pressed towards us. Already aware of the danger to our horses' foothold, this movement frightened me very much. The crowd along the roadside were within reach of our batons. As I rode on the outside and let mine swing on its thong from my wrist, I smiled as if I found these incidents amusing.

Actually they were I thought the most ticklish moments of the whole strike, for, determined action by the strikers might have brought many more of our horses down. Of this I was well aware! The crowd in front of us was the largest we had yet seen. They gave way before us when we moved on but kept up a great noise.

The lorries were eventually loaded and unlike Wellington, Auckland did not experience any violent rioting. Spencer's troop presented him with a silver cigar case and he returned to the King Country.

Life went on quietly for nearly nine months until August 1914. Then, the powder keg erupted. War began in Europe.

# War

---

On June 28, 1914, Archduke Franz-Ferdinand, heir to the Emperor of Austria-Hungary, was assassinated in Sarajevo by an Austrian trained in Serbia who belonged to a secret society called Black Hand. It ignited a gunpowder trail of international treaties. On July 28 Austria-Hungary declared war on Serbia. On July 30, Russia which backed Serbia, called a general mobilisation. On August 31, after Russia refused to stop mobilisation, Germany went to war with them. France mobilised after Germany invaded Luxembourg and demanded Belgium give it access for action against France. As the situation worsened Spencer made ready to go to an officer's course in Auckland.

Monday 3rd [August] I caught the train for Auckland. I was dressed in khaki uniform as I was travelling on a military warrant. The *New Zealand Herald* had arrived. I bought a copy and read it on the journey. It was quite interesting. There had been trouble near Dublin the previous week. A mob had attacked a party of the King's Own Scottish Borderers who had fired killing three and injuring thirty two. We had wondered in recent months how long British troops could keep their temper in the face of abuse and violence. Perhaps this would steady things down.

Austria Hungary had declared war on Serbia. Russia

was not satisfied it appeared either and might attack the Austrians. There was pessimism in England. But I could not see why. It was a Balkan affair. Let it stay there. Italy said she would be neutral. No doubt we would too. I did not believe the Liberal government in England would fight anyone, even if they ought. Still rumour was abroad in Wellington and the Dominion was said to be ready. The Irish strife was declared over. That was one good thing.

The train stopped in Te Awamutu for tea and contrary to what Spencer was thinking, everyone seemed to be saying there would be war. When he reached Auckland he went to the drill hall to find he had misread his orders and the course had started that morning.

He hurried off to the wharf to see the departure of men he knew who were going to England to join up. Next day he learned France had been invaded, that Canada had offered 30,000 men, that the Naval Reserve had been called up and the British fleet was at sea. War looked likely.

Even if we were not in it yet, there was a tense atmosphere of excitement waiting to break out in the streets and a kindly eye for those of us who happened to wear uniform, regardless of rank.

On August 4, the day after Spencer arrived in Auckland, Germany marched into Belgium. The Germans thought troubles in Ireland would keep Britain's hands full and that if she went to war, Ireland would stick a dagger in her back. But Britain did not back away and demanded the Germans stop. The call was ignored. To the Germans' surprise Britain declared war against them and to their annoyance Nationalist Catholics in the south of Ireland pledged their support to fight for Britain.

New Zealand was advised. The Governor, Lord Liverpool, announced the dire news to a crowd of over 15,000 in Wellington. As part of the British Empire, New Zealand was in the fight as well. Liverpool told the crowd the King expressed his thanks for the Dominion's fullest support in the present conflict. The news reached Auckland where Spencer continued on his course.

We discussed it in every aspect as we smoked our pipes in the spell periods between our work. We were most of us in my class, young enough to be eager to go but I was surprised to find there were some who weren't. It staggered me later to find officers in my billet, much my senior, especially two mounted rifle men who had no intention of going.

They must have been elected to commissions before the territorial force days and drilled and worn the uniform with no idea they would ever be expected to do so in action.

Captain Bluck

There was Captain Bluck that I had known in the strike. In the passage I heard him holding a long distance conversation with his wife. He had said he would be going and after a pause with the note of surprise in his voice he asked 'You are not crying. Are you?' I fled. Bluck was a dairy farmer with a young family. I felt he should not go.

Bluck, of 4 Waikato Squadron, Auckland Mounted Rifles, would be shot dead by a sniper on Russell's Top, Gallipoli, on May 18, 1915.

If he wanted, Spencer need not have volunteered either. But not to do so would have been unthinkable for the 28-year-old. Thousands of young men up and down the country were quick to volunteer. It was learned New Zealand would send an expeditionary force of four regiments of mounted rifles, four battalions of infantry with guns, engineers and other back-up.

Spencer sent an application form to his cousin Rupert who had left the navy and was working as an insurance clerk in Auckland. Rupert would join the Auckland infantry's HQ staff with the rank of lance corporal.

Spencer, meanwhile, filled out an application form himself also and joined up with his 16th Waikato Company which formed part of the Auckland Infantry Battalion. He went back to Te Kuiti where he assisted with enlistments.

The first volunteers, 1400 from Wellington and Auckland, were dispatched to annex German Samoa which was achieved bloodlessly. Spencer made his way back to Auckland where serious training began. He was not long in camp when a young Maori woman, named Kereihi, arrived from the King Country wanting to speak to him. She referred to him as "her cousin." How this came about was due to three sons of Spencer's great grandfather, the sculptor Sir Richard Westmacott, who spent time in New Zealand around 1840. One of them fathered a child by a Maori woman in the King Country. Kereihi presented Spencer with a greenstone tiki and a huia feather which she explained had been worn by chiefs in battle. He would wear them into action.

Rupert Westmacott

When given the chance for leave Spencer, accompanied by Rupert — now joined up — visited Mary and Esther Foster at their parents' home in Remuera. He and Mary agreed to marry. Only family and a few close friends knew.

The civilians in town treated every one with great kindness. We all got into mischief, falling in love or thinking we did being a common form, and perhaps from a military point of view the most harmless, though most of these affairs ended when the ships sailed. The men wrote now and again to the girls they left behind them.

One regrets when one looks back that most of those grand boys died childless. The universal treating to the men whenever they got a few hours furlough was a confounded nuisance. Their friends met them at the gate and escorted them into town where too many of them succumbed to the influence of the flowing bowl. To counteract this, strong squads of military police were formed to patrol the town and environs of the camp.

Route marches, attack practices squad and platoon drill filled the next weeks and soon became tiresome.

We reached a state where every day's delay seemed most galling. We considered ourselves in a high state of efficiency. Rifles had all been through the Armourers' hands and all equipment was subjected to constant and rigid inspection. Medical inspections of the most searching nature had been further carried out, barefoot parades were held and every possible contingency had been provided for whilst the officers even attended a daily class of fencing and swordsmanship under an old Army champion. We were completely equipped. Every man had two uniforms. Officers were armed with sword and revolver. We also wore Sam Browne belts, haversacks and water bottles each with their own straps, also field glasses. We carried message and order books.

Two grey transports lay at the wharf at the foot of Queen St. All the NZ transports at that date were painted Man-o-war grey. Further delays would occur but eventually a formal farewell was held in Auckland.

In due course the drums commenced to roll on the wharf and we fell in and marched off in the pouring rain. At the Domain we came into mass formation facing the grandstand where we were addressed by Mr Massey [Prime Minister William Massey] and a number of other people. No doubt the reporters got full reports which were published in the local papers probably.

The crowd was a large one and gazed upon us with interest. There was every indication of patriotic fervour. Loud cheers and 'God save the King.' The junior officers and men were bored and were anxious to get back on board ship. To stand an hour listening to speeches one cannot hear, with the rain trickling down one's rifle barrel is not so inspiring that the order to move is not welcomed and we were glad to go. As we were marching for the gate from the banked crowds above us a voice called to me 'Want a piper sir?' and a tall figure in tartans fell in beside me and played us down.

The companies each carried the colours of their parent regiments, the only occasion they ever did so. At the top of Queen Street Jack Mackay who had been with me on

Lieutenant Spencer Westmacott in camp.

a survey party in the Rangitoto and had fought in South Africa stepped forward shook me by the hand and in silence fell back in the crowd. The people were lined many deep all down the street to the wharf.

At one point I saw Mrs Foster who had shown me so much kindness and Mrs Bloomfield. To step aside shake them by the hand and regain the head of my platoon took barely ten seconds. There was little cheering now. Looking back presently I saw old Mr Clark of Otorohanga smoking furiously, marching in step in the ranks beside his son, and he passed with us onto the wharf where no one but soldiers were supposed to go.

Spencer then received orders to take 100 men by rail to Wellington to embark them there since one of the two troopships in Auckland was overcrowded. He rushed down and returned to Auckland where he boarded the troopship carrying his company among 1500 men and 500 horses. There were also numerous dogs which had been smuggled on board. Once this became known the Military Police scoured the ship, bundled them into a lighter and took them ashore. Three remained — the company mascot, Rewi, a sheep dog, and a mongrel that belonged to the ship called Pie Shop.

After a further delay due to a fear of enemy shipping, on October 11 the troopships sailed for Wellington to join the rest of the expeditionary force.

The stay in the capital was a short one and on October 16, the full expeditionary force, a massive group for such a small country — over 8000 men making up the NZ Mounted Rifle Brigade and NZ Infantry Brigade — sailed for what they thought would be Britain.

If Spencer felt any emotion about his departure, he kept it to himself. He was a soldier off to war and had no misgivings.

The New Zealand convoy called first at Hobart and then Albany at King George Sound in Western Australia where they linked up with the Australian Expeditionary Force's 27 troopships and continued on.

# Egypt … and an unlikely enemy

Training went on during the voyage. There was space on the exercise deck for two platoons to work on each side and this was done on a roster basis. The troops went through arms drill, physical drill and musketry. They stopped at Colombo and Aden before reaching the Suez Canal.

Our passage through the Suez Canal was one long thrill from the time we looked out at a large blur on the Sinai desert, saw steel flashing in the afternoon sun and realized they were troops, our own from the Indian Army.

Our [ship] captain nearly brought his feud with that of the Ruapehu [another troopship] to a murderous end by racing him for the entrance of the canal, but the Ruapehu won.

The canal was guarded by half battalion entrenched posts of the Indian Army at intervals along the eastern bank. As we came in rear of each we would call out, "Who are you?" and receive the reply, "A hundred and twenty eighth Pioneers Indian Army, and you?" in a British officer's voice. We did not realize they were as enthusiastic to be told "First Auckland regiment New Zealand" as we were to hear about them. It certainly made us feel we belonged to a mighty army.

At Port Said we steamed past several transports filled with Australians. From a distance we were struck with their discipline as they lined the decks. Their bugles would play "Attention" and every man sprang to that position at once and remained so till the call to "Carry on!" sent them all about their business again. We hoped we were being as good, though looking at our men close to, they did not look at all smart in the sea kit after their eight weeks voyage.

The convoy reached Alexandria on December 3, 1914, and the troops disembarked and boarded trains.

The un-travelled lack of sophistication of the New Zealander at that time was remarkable. In New Zealand the sale of liquor was strictly regulated and as voting returns would show, the shadow of prohibition was over the land. Not so in Egypt and it sounded very heinous when we were told that natives would even try to sell liquor openly to the men in the troop trains. We officers

Corporal Patterson
(later sergeant)

were instructed that this liquor was rank poison so when, having entrained the men on Alexandria wharf, I went along outside the carriages and saw a tall man of mine called Alec Patterson from Kinohaku looking at a bottle of whiskey, I snatched it from him and smashed it against the wheel of the carriage saying, "I am surprised at you Patterson. You know the orders are for no one to buy liquor from natives."

"But I didn't buy it, sir," he said. "I was only looking at it. It was got up like Black and White whiskey and I believe it was."

So, I now think it was, and that the wretched native

vendor, who loudly protested, was breaking no law, and lost the price of good Scotch whiskey besides the profit on a sale.

Going into the carriage which carried most of my platoon, I found the men with open bottles drinking happily, in their seats. Most of the [beer] bottles were by now half empty and the men having had eight weeks teetotalism through the tropics one could hardly stop them drinking something now. If I took drastic action against these I could see they would only be more secret about it and get it in spite of us. As it turned out, it was the real stuff and did no one on the train a bit of harm.

Scottish-born Alec Patterson, 31, by then a sergeant, would die of wounds at Gallipoli on May 22, 1915.

After their train journey Spencer and the New Zealand soldiers settled into their new home, Zeitoun, a camp 10km north-east of Cairo.

The New Zealand camp at Zeitoun.

With the 4th Australian Infantry Brigade and 1st Australian Light Horse brigade they combined to form the NZ and Australian Division comprising a force of more than 17,000. Australia's war correspondent, Charles Bean, described it as a marriage of convenience to make up a division. Major-General Sir Alexander Godley, who had overseen New Zealand's military forces before the war, was placed in command.

Together with the 1st Australian Division they were formed into an army corps of two divisions commanded by Lieutenant General Sir William Birdwood, who had served on the North Western Frontier in India under Spencer's uncle, General Dick Westmacott, and had a distinguished career in the Anglo-Boer War.

Major-General Godley

ANZAC was adopted as the corps telegraphic address and was soon in wide usage as the term to describe the New Zealanders and Australians.

When they left New Zealand most troops had hoped to spend Christmas in England. Once in Egypt, however, Godley announced the force would train there for a period before continuing on to England.

What had transpired was Britain's First Lord of the Admiralty, Winston Churchill, had requested that the Australians and New Zealanders stay in Egypt in case they were required for action in the Dardanelles. Churchill was determined that the Allies (Britain, France) take Constantinople[1] as a way to bring a prompt end to the war.

The improbable scenario had emerged that the New Zealanders would be fighting not Germans on the Western Front which in just over four months had already become a depressing stalemate with half the British Army destroyed, but Turks.

Formerly a traditional ally of Britain, Turkey and its Ottoman Empire had joined forces with the German and Austro-Hungarian

---

1 Constantinople, the then capital of Turkey, is now called Istanbul. In 1923 the Turkish capital was moved to Ankara.

Empires, the Central Powers, against the British, French and Russians and shut off the strategically important Straits of the Dardanelles — thereby separating Russia from her allies and depriving her of vital supplies as well as the main route through which all its grain and half its exports passed. Russia's nightmare was to have Germany in charge of the Straits.

Turkey's close relationship with Germany followed a long drawn out process of wars, revolutions and diplomatic intrigue. Once the most powerful state in the world stretching from the Atlantic shore of North Africa to the borders of Iran, Austria, Poland and Russia, the Ottoman Empire had been declining since reaching its peak in the seventeenth century.

At the top as absolute monarch presiding over this Muslim styled empire of 22 million people about half of whom were ethnic Turks, the rest Greeks, Kurds, Armenians and dozens of tribal minorities, sat the Sultan, successor of Muhammed.

The empire had flirted with a parliamentary constitution in 1876 but this had been quickly abandoned after the Ottomans went to war with Russia. Major change came only in 1908 when a party of reformists and military officers — the Committee of Union and Progress Party (CUP) — known in the West as the Young Turks, proclaimed open revolt against Sultan Abdul Hamid II, or as he was sometimes called, Abdul the Damned. They wanted to slash the influence of Islam, create a Western style democracy and develop a sense of Turkish nationalism.

Such was their power, Abdul the Damned reintroduced the parliamentary constitution and was forced to abdicate peacefully.

Then came more turmoil: Instead of preventing the disintegration of the empire as the CUP had hoped, their revolutionary spirit sparked a counter revolution in the empire's Balkan territories. Austria, in defiance of a treaty with the empire, annexed the Turkish provinces of Bosnia and Herzegovina which as mentioned nearly sent Europe to war; Crete voted to join up with Greece, Bulgaria, yet another part of the fading empire, proclaimed independence.

Next, in 1911 Italy occupied the Turkish provinces of Tripoli and

Cyrenaica in North Africa sparking a war with the Ottoman Empire which the Turks lost.

In 1912 Christian Balkan states – Greece, Bulgaria, Serbia and Montenenegro – joined forces and also declared war on the empire. It became known as the first Balkan War. Almost as expected things went depressingly for the Turks.

A proposed armistice would have the Ottoman Government give away all Balkan provinces. Outraged at this, a group of CUP members led by a vain and dapper 32-year-old army officer, Enver Pasha, shot dead the Minister of War Nazim Pasha and forced by gunpoint the head of the government, Kamil Pasha, to resign.

The group demanded the Sultan appoint Mahmud Sevket to replace Kamil. This happened. The war ended in humiliation – almost all of Ottoman Europe was lost and subsequently Mahmud Sevket was assassinated and his 12 alleged killers hanged.

No sooner had the war ended when Christian Balkan states – Greece, Bulgaria and Serbia – started arguing over the spoils and Bulgaria linked up with Rumania against Greece and Serbia in the Second Balkan War.

On this occasion the Turks kept out of it except for a peaceful reoccupation of Adrianople. When the war ended Germany started to court the three Ottoman leaders, Enver, Ahmed, the Minister for Navy, and Talat, a former telegraph operator and the Minister of the Interior. Germany had already had a strong influence in the empire with a military mission having been established in 1882. In December 1913 Enver invited German general Otto von Sanders to head another military mission in Turkey and in effect von Sanders became commander of an Ottoman army corps stationed, to the consternation of Russia, at the Straits. It has been claimed this appointment marked the real start of the countdown to the beginning of World War One.

In July 1914 Austria declared war on Serbia and Winston Churchill raised the issue of two Turkish battleships that were then being built in Britain. The Young Turks agreed, meanwhile, that if Germany provided more than two million pounds to support their military they would enter a defensive alliance with them against Russia.

On August 2 the Turks laid mines in the Straits of the Dardanelles and Churchill responded by confiscating the two Turkish battleships being built in Newcastle. Britain declared war on Germany and the Royal Navy pursued two German vessels trapped in the Mediterranean — a battle cruiser *Goeben* and light cruiser, *Breslau*. The Germans appealed to the Turks to allow the ships to enter the Dardanelles and safety. The Turks agreed and once the ships reached the Dardanelles declared they had purchased them from Germany.

All of this was considered provocative to the British. The final act which brought Turkey into the war, however, came late in October when the Ottoman fleet under the command of a German bombarded Russian Black Sea ports. At once Russia declared war on the Ottoman Empire followed by Britain and France.

The British Foreign Office outlined its view of events on November 1, 1914, in a report published in most New Zealand newspapers:

At the beginning of the war the British Government gave definite assurance that if Turkey remained neutral her independence and integrity would be respected during the war and in the terms of peace. In this Russia concurred.

A postcard of Constantinople at the time of the Gallipoli campaign, sent from Constantinople to Germany.

On October 29, the British Government learnt with the utmost regret that Turkish ships of war had without any declaration of war and without warning or provocation, of any sort, made wanton attacks upon an undefended town on the Black Sea of a friendly country, thus committing an unprecedented violation of the most ordinary rule of international law, equity and usage.

Ever since the *Goeben* and *Breslau* took refuge in Constantinople the attitude of the Turkish government towards the British had caused surprise and uneasiness. Promises were made by the Turkish Government to send away the German officers and crews of the *Goeben* and *Breslau* but never fulfilled. It is well known that the Turkish Minister of War [Enver] was decidedly pro-German but it was confidently hoped that the saner counsels of his colleagues who have experience of the friendship which Great Britain had always shown towards the Turkish Government, would prevail.

Since the war began German officials in large numbers have invaded Constantinople and usurped the authority of the government and have been able to coerce the Sultan's ministers into taking a policy of aggression vigorously assisted by the Ambassador of Germany and Austria [Wangenheim].

German military elements in Constantinople have been persistently doing their utmost to force Turkey into the war, both by their activities in the service of the Turks, and by lavish bribes. (*Ashburton Guardian*, November 3, 1914)

Many Turks were reluctant to go to war. Also, most of the Ottoman cabinet resigned protesting against Enver's pro-German stance and part in provoking Russia into a war. Regardless Turkey was in the war.

To the New Zealanders in Egypt it would come as a surprise to learn that the first soldiers they would fight would not be Germans, but Turks.

# Training in earnest

Such was the background to Turkey's entry into the war.

For Spencer and the New Zealanders if they knew of it at all, their knowledge was gleaned from sketchy newspaper reports. Having settled in at Zeitoun, it was now on to a harder grind of training.

> We commenced training again in earnest. I say 'again' for we had already, we thought, been trained in New Zealand. But that had been easy to what we had to undergo. However, we first commenced with a smartening up process. Someone said there was nothing like squad drill for this. But we did not mind the work entailed and even derived some fun out of our life and daily round. This is understandable when I say that Allen, Baddeley and myself were rarely found fault with, another officer being the whipping boy.

Spencer's fellow company lieutenants, Harold Allen, aged 21, and Stuart Baddeley, 23, would be his closest companions during their time in Egypt. Both would die at Gallipoli on April 25, 1915. Spencer had much in common with them.

Liverpool-born Allen was a farm cadet and shared Spencer's regard for the military having spent two years at the Royal Military College, Duntroon, in Australia. He had been educated at King's College in Auckland. His reason for leaving Duntroon Spencer did not know.

Baddeley had attended Victoria University, Wellington, and worked as a solicitor in Te Awamutu. Spencer found him to be honest, clever and athletic.

Lieutenant Morgan

All three were idealistic and patriotic. Spencer, the oldest at 28, was the guiding and almost fatherly influence among them.

The whipping boy he referred to was 35-year-old Lieutenant Harry Morgan, a self-employed Auckland estate and land agent. Morgan had emigrated from England to New Zealand in 1891 and was married with a three-year-old daughter.

He [Morgan] had travelled over in the same troopship as the Canterbury regiment in charge of part of our first reinforcement. One gathered that he had early attracted the Canterbury battalion commander Colonel Macbean Stewart's attention there for not being orthodox and somewhat casual. With most of us he would disarm criticism by a pleasant smile and ready admission of any fault but Colonel Stewart, like Colonel Malone of the Wellingtons, was rigidly orthodox and very strict, looking to find fault he soon found it. On the first occasion Morgan missed a lecture held for all officers, Stewart had sent for him and asked for an explanation to be told.

"Sir, I am very sorry, but I was writing a letter to my wife and overlooked the time until it was really too late so I thought I had better remain away."

He smiled engagingly.

Stewart would appear to have smiled too — he had a sense of humour — not so engagingly perhaps but quite politely as he said.

"Very good Mr Morgan. Three days extra orderly duty."

"Thank you, sir," said Morgan repeating the anecdote to me. There seemed nothing else I could say.

Spencer believed Morgan failed as a platoon commander even though he was energetic and keen. Morgan would become the battalion's transport officer. Lt-Colonel Macbean Stewart, 38, was married with three children and worked as a shipping agent and accountant in civilian life. He would be shot through the head and killed on April 25, 1915. Lt-Colonel Malone, 53, lawyer and farmer, would become arguably New Zealand's greatest hero at Gallipoli for his actions on Chunk Bair in August. Three of his sons would serve at Gallipoli. Malone would be killed by Royal Naval shelling during August.

Colonel Malone wearing his distinctive 'Lemon-squeezer' hat which was later adopted by the NZ Army as its official head-dress.

The rigours of training were suspended on December 23 when the New Zealand troops, together with other Allied forces, marched in a display of strength to a central part of Cairo where Lieutenant General Sir John Maxwell, commander in chief of the forces in Egypt, took the salute.

Britain had formally annexed Egypt as a protectorate of its empire and the march was designed to dampen down pro-Turkish sentiment as Egyptian newspapers described the Turks as preparing to make a bid for the Suez Canal. A Khedive ruled Egypt but he had gone to Constantinople and thrown his support behind the Turks and Germans.

The British appointed the Khedive's elderly uncle in his place. Spencer said the march was "a celebration of the new protectorate and to demonstrate our power to any unruly element who might feel like giving trouble." In the native quarter they encountered looks of "smouldering impotent hatred," but he did not realize that General Maxwell was present when they came to the saluting point approaching the Shepheards Hotel near the Ezbekieh Gardens.

We got "eyes right!" Before we knew we were saluting General [Birdwood] and his staff on their horses and then like a snapshot we took in the presence of the Australian Light Horse, long lines of them sitting immobile in their saddles, their rifles resting butt on thigh at the 'carry;' horses and men, each superb as one, the only movement being the occasional throw high of a proud animal's head and the toss of a shiny mane. This was the Australia we had dreamed about and by now never thought to see.

Christmas Day was marked with a welcome day off training; soon after Spencer's batman disappeared.

I lost my batman little MacLean [sic].[1] It was the custom whilst we remained in company messes for one batman to remain on duty till last post clearing away and washing up after the evening meal and then rolling our bedding down.

Being orderly officer on Xmas day I found MacLean employed in this duty, sympathized with him and gave him one of my golden sovereigns as a Xmas box. He thanked me and disappeared for three days after which he got 14 days in the Citadel and I had to get a new batman, Arthur Fish from Marakopa taking on this duty for me. Old Tom Lahy had already done a turn in the Citadel [a castle used as military prison] for being Absent Without Leave and on return had most amusing stories to tell of it, of the coarse abuse and terrifying behaviour of the NCOs in charge there who all appeared to be, as the situation required, the toughest in the army.

"I'll pass my left to your jaw if you don't jump when you're spoken to my lad," was a mild threat from them and apparently they did jump, even though they felt murderous about it. Old Lahy said they gave a real training to a man once inside the Citadel, no humbug or by your leave. "It's what 'arf these young fellers need," said he and with a

---

1 This is 12/811 Private Philip McLean. Glasgow-born McLean would be wounded at Gallipoli and in France. He was discharged from the army December 1917.

pleased smile. "I hear young MacLean's been sent there, and a good thing for 'im too sir. It's just what he needs. E aint got no idea. Too cheeky altogether 'e is; but they'll make a soldier of 'im there."

Private Fish, aged 26, was a self-employed bushman in civilian life and would have a long association with Spencer. Private Lahy, a cook in New Zealand, would marry in Alexandria while convalescing from wounds. In 1917 he was discharged from the army on account of a pre-enlistment disability aggravated on active service.

Meanwhile, the British were preparing for naval attacks on the Dardanelles Straits after having already made a preliminary assault during early November in which the outer forts had been bombarded for about 10 minutes to find the range of the Turkish fort guns. The attack merely forewarned the Turks who started defending the Gallipoli peninsula which already had defensive works dating back centuries.

Spencer Westmacott's men had to train on New Year's Day, marching five miles into the desert which led to much grumbling.

These defences had since been improved during the First Balkan War. Yet the Dardanelles was only one front upon which the Turks had to focus. British forces had gained a foothold in Mesopotamia and on December 29 in their first major offensive of the war, the Turks had sent a 100,000 strong army into the Caucasus which was mauled by the Russians at the Battle of Sarikamish in what would prove one of the greatest military disasters of the twentieth century.

After this slaughter, New Zealand newspapers reported Constantinople was covered in posters inciting the populace to punish the Germans for pushing them into the war. Other reports said the Turks were threatening to massacre their Christian population should the Allies force their way through the Dardanelles Straits (presently Strait) and that they were already slaughtering Armenians, partly as a result of Armenians fighting with the Russians against them. A London report published in New Zealand newspapers quoted a Turkish colonel telling a Bourse correspondent that Enver had been Turkey's ruin.

"This wretched brainless puppet of the Kaiser has brought Turkey to a position of imperilling the Ottoman Empire. There is no Turkey now — only a German province." (*Ashburton Guardian*, January 4, 1915)

# Enthusiasm wanes

The New Zealand troops were also a little less enthusiastic. Spencer:

> The fact is, the first enthusiasm for each other and the joy of being together on active service had modified, we had trained so hard, were still doing so that we would have been all the better for being 'a little shooted.' We nursed grievances. McDonald had one.

Captain McDonald, an accountant of Frankton Junction, was acting company commander and would, to his chagrin, later be overlooked for the position when a permanent appointment was made.

> He had worked the company hard. He was a small man and a real martinet. It may sound ridiculous, but the men were more afraid of him than they seemed likely to be of any enemy. The consequence was they were always on their toes when he was about and the result was a very smart company.
>
> New Year's Day was not a holiday either; the men were all unhappy at having to train and trouble arose.
>
> Everyone one was in a bad temper at having to work New Year's Day. The syllabus was not a heavy one but commenced with a march out of over five miles, of course in full pack. Captain McDonald supervised the parade of

the company and then saying he would go ahead of us and fix the position of our halting place he handed over to me and rode off. I gave the order "Advance in column of route from the right, number thirteen platoon leading." Allen gave the word, "Number thirteen — form fours — right — By the left — left wheel — Quick march."

The others followed in succession. We came out on the road through the camp, marched along it at the slope until we emerged from the tented area and came on to the desert sand, when from the head of the column where I was marching I gave the order "March at ease" which passed down the fours, the men slinging their rifles as they got it. Old Sergeant Major Hobbs as he did so said to me, "Well! It does seem hard, sir to have to go for a route march on New Year's Day."

Up to this time I had shared this feeling with my

brother officers. Now I realized that we must not express it, and I said, "Sergeant Major, a soldier has to do as he is told. So it is no use talking about it."

"Oh yes sir," he replied, and without further complaint loyally bore himself cheerfully.

Sergeant Major Hobbs, an Englishman from Kincott, Berkshire, was 56. He had given his age as 44 when he enlisted.

Sergeant Major Hobbs

Under a quarter of an hour from moving off, we arrived at the high sand embankment of the old Suez railway where I halted the company and the men lay back on their packs whilst we three officers Baddeley, Allen and I climbed the bank, spread our maps on it, opened our compasses, set them and took stock of the scenery.

Land marks were scarce but we got a bearing onto a

place in Heliopolis to our right and another on to a water tower to our left rear, ruled them in on the map with our protractors, found our position and then took a bearing of the way we had to go.

Flat featureless desert lay before us but we knew our direction now and another hour and a half of marching would bring us to our ground.

Back to the company we went, called the men up and marched off again. Sergeant Major Hobbs and many of the men were smoking now. Cigarettes were not allowed, it being believed they impaired the wind on the march, but pipes were, and no doubt a few draws at his briar had put the Sergeant Major into a philosophical frame of mind.

In all his years of service in the Scots Guards he must have had to do many things he had not liked, hard marching was no new experience for him. The infantry had had much of it in the South African war. I was feeling more cheerful too. It is a curious thing, perhaps a sign of combativeness in human nature, that though I had fallen in a state of discontent like the rest, the fact that I was aware that our 250 NCOs and men had probably never paraded in a more resentful mutinous state than they did that morning, only made me the more determined to hold them to their duty.

As we marched though, it was apparent still, that the sense of grievance had by no means disappeared. Usually our good country boys were cheerful enough. They commented on the scenery and the turn-out of other troops, and pulled each other's legs. Young West from Fencourt near Cambridge was often the recipient of most astounding information that made me smile inwardly.

Private West

"Terrible country this in winter, Westy." I heard Private Nicholson say one day as his eye roamed over the endless flat, with ridges and gullies stretching to the limit of vision. It was sand, pebbles and an occasional thorn in every direction.

"Aw?" said West enquiringly.

"Yes. All under water now." The sun was shining and West was blissfully unaware that it was mid-winter now in the northern hemisphere.

There was none of this banter today. The likes of Nicholson with his north Irish blood and moody temper were tramping on in surly silence. It was on such an occasion that one could study the variety of disposition in the company. Some were grumbling, audibly unless one looked at them, others with a sort of vague undercurrent, nothing one could take hold of, whilst for the most part the men tramped with a puzzled expression. It was obvious that no one was happy. As the march continued some pointedly began to ask each other the time and presently I heard voices enquire, but not too loudly. "What about a halt?" "We ought to have a halt by now."

From the time we had left the parade ground in camp was now just on fifty minutes, and had we marched continuously ever since, I was bound, by the regulations for march discipline to halt and rest for ten minutes, but I was now myself resentful and certainly not going to be influenced by malcontents. We had halted and rested for over five minutes at the Suez railway whilst looking at the maps and I meant to count my marching time from there, so kept them going for another five minutes. The protests were audible but I could not detect the men who voiced them when I turned to see, and in spite of it the men kept on marching.

At this moment Sergeant Pearse came up from the left rear. His face looked red and ill tempered. He had had his full share of the New Year's Eve beer. He always could carry it well enough to pass muster but now no doubt he was suffering a reaction as he addressed Hobbs in an angry voice saying, "Sergeant Major! How much longer is this going on? We should have halted five minutes ago. The men are being over marched and are falling out all over the place."

Before Hobbs could reply I had turned on him and said, "I am in command of the company, sergeant. Go back to your place."

He went off. I had to halt but it was with reluctance I did so though my time was up. In view of Pearse's behaviour I would gladly have continued further. Instead, as the men relaxed to the ground, I went away to the flank of the resting column and called the officers to me and when they had come up I asked if the men were all right. They said they were but for the grumbling and some had fallen out. Asking how Pearse had behaved Baddeley said he had been a nuisance, complaining about slave driving and forced marches in the hearing of the men and creating discontent to such an extent that he had himself fallen back to the two rear sections where Pearse was and done his best to encourage everyone to keep on.

"Set me a falling out state from each platoon," said I, "and send Pearse up to me." The others went off on their errand and presently Pearse arrived marching smartly at the slope. He slapped the small of his butt correctly as he halted three paces from me, but there was defiance in the way he did it.

"Sergeant Pearse," said I, "Did you get permission from your platoon commander to come up to the head of the company just now?"

"No sir," he replied, "I didn't know I had to."

"Well, it is news to me if an NCO can go wandering about at his own will. Fall back to your place."

He saluted but he looked less defiant and more serious as he went off.

Baddeley and Allen and the sergeants temporarily in charge of the other two platoons now reported. From the three leading platoons two men had fallen out. From Baddeley's eight had done so, and these were all from the two rear sections where Pearse had been. This was a pretty damning piece of evidence.

I determined to make an example of him. He had been undermining Baddeley his officer where it had been his duty to support him all he knew.

The ex-NCOs of the British Regular Army understood this relationship and their influence was a tower of strength to the NZEF. But of course if Pearse or anyone else could go on in this way it would undermine discipline.

The proceedings during this halt occupied some little time. Those members of the company not concerned with that uncanny instinct no one can explain had at once sensed that something unusual was happening, this had awakened their curiosity and the result was we now marched in quite a good humour.

Pearse had his own thoughts to keep him quiet. When we reached Macdonald [sic] standing by his horse, he congratulated me on the steady way they were all marching. I was pleased and then I told him the events of the morning. He agreed when I said I was bringing Pearse before him at company orderly room, but asked what I could charge him with.

"Conduct to the prejudice of good order and military discipline," said I.

Before we dismissed I said Pearse was to come to me afterwards and when he came up said, "Sergeant I am reporting what occurred this morning."

"Oh, why sir?" he enquired politely and correctly.

"Because we would have no discipline at all if we let that kind of thing go on," I told him.

Poor Pearse! He came before McDonald when everyone had had time to wash and brush up half an hour later. I told my story. Baddeley told his.

Asked what he had to say he pleaded "not guilty." His knees were shaking as he turned towards me and said, "I am sure Mr Westmacott does not wish to proceed with this charge. The season of the year, sir?"

It was very distressing and a plea I was eager to listen to. Instead I thought of Baddeley's troubles and was hard. "I have stated the case Sergeant," I said.

McDonald was firm too, saying, "This is too serious to be overlooked sergeant. I cannot deal with it. It must go before the commanding officer."

Colonel Plugge was amiable and weak. He hated trouble in his battalion. Pearse called evidence as to time we left camp and time we halted, omitting to mention our halt at the old Suez railway.

He asked me, "What did I say to you, sir. When I came up to the front of the company?"

"You did not speak to me sergeant," I told him. "You addressed the sergeant major."

Colonel Plugge

But of course the most damning evidence against him was the fact that eight men had fallen out where he was marching.

"Severely reprimanded," said the colonel.

We thought he should have sent him for court martial but it was serious for one of the permanent staff and it brought Pearse to his senses. He was a model soldier ever after.

Pearse, like Private West, would be killed in action on April 25, 1915. Auckland battalion commander Colonel Plugge, an English-born science teacher at Auckland's King's College, would be wounded on April 25 and again in May 1915. Plugge's Plateau immediately west of Anzac Cove, where he established his HQ on April 25, would be named for him. He would be mentioned twice in dispatches and made Companion of St Michael and St George.

# Australians 'boastful and noisy'

The Australians were in camp about 15 miles from Zeitoun and generally the New Zealanders only met up with them when on leave in Cairo. Now far from home soldiers from both forces indulged in the temptations the city could offer. The Australians indulged the most and quickly acquired a reputation for drunkenness. Fights between New Zealand and Australian soldiers were frequent.

Spencer was impressed by the Australian Light Horse, but not so the Australian infantry; attitudes which would change.

Up to now we had seen little of the Australians at their work and had formed a very poor opinion of them when we met them on leave, when they thronged the streets of Cairo and seemed to us very boastful and noisy. We wished to be in no way associated with them.

Yet coming through the canal [en route to Egypt] several troopships we passed had impressed us by the smartness with which all men on deck came to 'Attention' as the bugle blew that call. We had been told these men were from New South Wales and that they had a very fine young brigadier called MacLaurin.

Whatever smartness they might have arrived with, soon seemed to vanish in Cairo where they gave way visibly to the temptations afforded by the flesh pots of Egypt.

It could not be said that our officers and men behaved like plaster saints either, but they seemed naturally quieter and our military police apprehended individuals who misbehaved conspicuously whilst check was carefully kept at the railway stations and in camp by pickets and guards on all men returning late from leave, or absent without it.

The latter was sufficiently bad for all leave to be stopped some days whilst the military police went systematically through the lower haunts of Cairo routing out anyone found there. It was said they got over 200 Australians and three New Zealanders.

Of course the various troops in Egypt in our vicinity interested us. The nearest were the 42nd Lancashire Territorial Division that our men immediately called the Tommies. They were well uniformed in khaki drill with helmets, a kit that we all envied them, we being still in the serge in which we left New Zealand and not the best for the desert.

Most of us officers purchased khaki drill and slacks which we wore with helmets when on leave. The suit cost 125 piastres, about 25 shillings of our money. Colonel Malone of the Wellington Regt. who with Colonel Macbean Stewart of Canterbury was the strictest, most orthodox and best of the COs in our brigade, would not let his officers wear anything but their own uniform even off parade and found fault with me in the train to Cairo for being improperly dressed, in which, of course he was quite right.

The Lancashire lads, mill hands mostly when at home, we were told, were small by comparison with our men, and then there were the British yeomanry of which there was a brigade. The latter, both officers and men were the flower of England, led by the aristocracy.

For some time the officers continued to carry the overcoat rolled over the left shoulder — but it was hotter that way — and water bottle and haversack.

Instead of the rifle and bayonet we had sword and revolver. We were allowed a kit bag of blankets and spare clothing weighing 35 pounds on the transport, no more. NCOs and men carried in addition to overcoat, blanket, waterproof sheet, water and rations, rifle and bayonet and 150 rounds of ball ammunition. These things with other odds and ends made up the load on the individual to over 60 pounds weight.

Our amusements when on leave in Cairo were not very edifying. We took our fun where we found it, dined together once a week at Shepheards on Saturday nights when we could and made a night of it as single men free from care. We did not know it but we were the worse for not being in contact with any home life whatever.

As for the advantages of being an officer, no doubt they were many. We were proud of our position, but it carried extra obligations and responsibility too and we took our share of "hard lying" and, when in company messes, stew from the Dixie too.

Fortunate were we in our Brigadier Earl Johnson [sic] who at that time we thought so much of a gentleman as to doubt if he was hard enough with us but we came to realize he had the measure of his battalion commanders.

Temperley was also a gentleman, no doubt of that, and the staff captain Morton of the NZ Staff Corps was as nice a fellow as one could wish, very good looking and well turned out and as events were to prove, brave as a lion.

History, however, has not looked upon these English officers, Johnston and Temperley so favourably. Johnston, the NZ Infantry Brigade commander later killed in action in France in August 1917, would be criticised by the British official historian for inept leadership at Gallipoli and during the August offensive at Chunuk Bair. The historian concluded: "It was a national calamity the he was allowed to continue command." (from *Damn The Dardanelles*, by John Laffin, Osprey Publishing,

London, 1980, p. 203) Temperley, another English loan officer with NZ Divisional HQ, would unfairly allege Colonel Malone, the Wellingtons' commander of compromising the chances of successfully defending Chunuk Bair. Malone did not like him. Captain Morton would die of wounds at Gallipoli on May 3, 1915.

The work grew hard enough now to begin to find out the weak links in our chain of discipline and we had to put the strain on and strengthen up.

Baddeley had trouble with some of his men. He was a grand young officer of a generous, open disposition who did not at first believe that he had anyone in the ranks who could play him false.

But he had a small group, several of whom had been drafted to him in Auckland who were the veriest riff raff. These did not improve a platoon drawn from the northern end of our district including Otahuhu and Huntly. He had begun by taking Nicholson as his batman, or the latter had taken to him. But he was far too strong a character to serve long in that capacity having a temper easily upset.

Baddeley had begun by leading his men much as a footballer leads a rugby team. He began to make up lost ground by checking every misdemeanour and 'criming' the culprits.

Some men at a halt, dissatisfied with some oranges sold them, upset the seller's basket and commenced picking their own. The general scramble was disorderly when Baddeley came down on them and crimed the chief offenders. They were not stealing as they meant to pay the man. But such things cannot be permitted lest they lead on to worse and the men were given CB.[1] Nicholson was amongst them. There was obvious resentment.

[Not long after] The company had been out on a long day's work and the heat was quite trying enough already

1 Confined to barracks.

for the time of year. At the end of a halt, on falling in, there was noticeable slackness. We were on the march home. We all called our men up to attention, stood them at ease and made them do it again. Most of them needed no more than that to spring to it properly.

But the group near the centre of Baddeley's platoon were not quick enough and Baddeley spoke to a man named Hagan who scowled and muttered at him, Baddeley had his name taken as we moved off.

This Hagan was a Liverpool Irishman who had been a ship's fireman and helped stoke the ship coming over on the *Waimana* where I had noticed him and he told me he had been in the Old Militia in England. He had been always very respectful to me, but I was not his platoon officer.

As soon as we arrived in camp Hagan was marched into the orderly room tent where McDonald was waiting to deal with delinquents. An attempt was made by his defending officer to make capital out of this afterwards, the contention being that he should have been kept till next morning to cool down.

McDonald listened to Baddeley's evidence; Hagan scowling ferociously had nothing to say and was awarded seven days CB. The sergeant major gave the order "prisoner and escort — right turn."

The escort complied but Hagan instead turned to the left and taking a step forward hit Baddeley in the jaw.

The latter, who could use his fists, quite naturally drew back his right, to strike back and might have done so for the man behind Hagan in the escort was a rather silly, undecided kind of fellow. But like a flash the corporal, Mettrick, collared Hagan round the neck and fell to the ground with him, where the man saying "It's all right Jim" lay quietly until allowed to get up, all the temper seemed to go out of him having struck the blow.

There was no question of releasing him now. Striking an officer was an offence that could, on active service, be punished by death. Hagan after being remanded to the colonel was marched off to the guard tent where he told everyone he intended to shoot Baddeley at the first opportunity.

When brought before the CO [Colonel Plugge] the latter had no option but to remand him to a general court martial, a thing that for the honour of his battalion he always hated doing, and seemed in no hurry to do so now.

Hagan, a printer from Huntly, was sent back to New Zealand, arriving the week the first casualty lists from Gallipoli were published in newspapers. He was jailed with hard labour and discharged from the army "with ignominy," on September 14, 1916.

# The NCOs

The desire of many of the New Zealanders was to be in action in France. As their days in Egypt dragged on, they were being referred to as 'Bill Massey's tourists'. But they were training hard.

We marched and marched. The third Auckland company had a song into which they often broke as the day wore on. It began:

Marching! Marching! Marching! Always bloody well marching! to the hymn tune Holy! Holy! Holy! We did not encourage it, partly because they sang it and partly because our country boys, though our language might seem to belie it, had an underlying reverence and an uneasy feeling it might be blasphemous to apply such words to religious music.

On these marches the steady pace was set for the company by old Hobbs, the company sergeant major.

On the occasions I was in charge temporarily and marched at the head I was inclined to step out, not so Hobbs who always maintained the regulation pace. More than once if I fell to day dreaming I have found myself unconsciously many yards ahead and this did not influence Hobbs in any way who with the habit of years never lengthened his pace which was good for the men, and when I woke up I would drop back to him.

He never changed expression on such occasions though I would see the leading fours grinning broadly. All ranks had an immense respect for him. He deserved it. We could wish for no more respectable man. His keeping of timetable and duty roster, for guards and fatigues never was wrong. He had a fine presence, red brown hair and moustache, stood over six feet, but so well-proportioned he did not look it.

Unlike so many of his rank one never noticed him on parade but he was always at the right spot. Our army owes an immeasurable debt to such men. Withal he was most exemplary. He could not have gone in for much dissipation on his rare leaves which he usually took in the evenings. His one indulgence was his pipe which he smoked a good deal, invariably lighting it when the order came to march at ease.

Hobbs had joined the permanent New Zealand army in 1911. He was described in staff records in 1913 as a very good all round soldier "but apt to talk too much on parade, lacks initiative and rather prone to magnify difficulties." Spencer:

My platoon sergeant Ward was as reliable as Hobbs and as respectable. I would no more have used bad language in front of him than I would to a woman. I used it very little in any case, but he would have shamed me.

My leading section was commanded by Sergeant Bennett. He was an ex-Kings Royal Rifle man having done his time, been in the South African War and finished his reserve time too. Quite a steady man, I believe he had been a barman in civil life who had more than once had to put Private Rhodes of mine, not so steady, out of his bar in the course of his duty. His discharge as corporal from the regulars had got him his sergeant's stripes. I think he must have been an orderly room corporal in the British Army.

Corporal Hathaway, an ex-marine, never failed me and should have been the sergeant. Steady and intelligent, his section always worked well and were a very happy family known as the singing section. Amongst them was Martin Daly [sic], a pardoned deserter from the Durham Light Infantry. Daly was a Roman Catholic and I suppose of Irish stock but he looked like a fair haired round headed Englishman. A good soldier, he proved able second to Hathaway when needed but he would never take stripes and I felt it would not pay to press one on him.

Corporal Hathaway, a bootmaker and labourer of Hamilton and a married man with two daughters aged six and one, would be promoted to sergeant on board the *Lutzow* shortly before the landing on April 25, 1915. He would be wounded in action August 8, 1915, and die in 1922.

Private Daley, a labourer, gave his next-of-kin as care of Barnados Homes, London. He would be discharged from the army in April 1918 due to asthma.

Grant, corporal of number three, was a good little man. He made a good section out of a rather mixed group of men, including Arthur Clarke of Otorohanga who was a bit of a wag whose humour was often, I knew directed at his corporal but not in a way I could take hold of.

His men called Grant 'The Bite' as he never hesitated to find fault and not being quite sure of himself, did so in a peremptory way. The slight doubt about his own fitness

Corporal Grant

did him no harm. Indeed it acted as a spur to him and arose from the doctor twice rejecting him for lack of chest expansion before I enlisted him.

Grant, aged 21, had been one of the first in the King Country attempting to enlist when war was announced. He was assistant engineer to the electric supply works for Otorohonga and Spencer wrote elsewhere had "a dark fiery eye." He would die of wounds from Gallipoli in Egypt on July 1, 1915.

There were times on long, testing marches when stronger men fell out from exhaustion, not many but an occasional man near breaking point. It was suggested to Grant once that he do so, but he said. "No! If I give in, it will be my last chance. Mr Westmacott knows me and that I had difficulty passing the doctor. He would send me back home if I ever gave in." I would not have done so then for there was fire in his dark eyes that I felt was invincible.

His men recognized Grant's dauntless spirit and despite the undercurrent of 'chipping' about him to each other of which he, like me, was aware, they respected and I believe, liked him.

Lastly, my fourth section was commanded by Corporal Eames. I had got him his stripes because of his South African medal ribbon and previous service in the Munsters. He won his men in the beginning when he took over and enquired their names telling them they must do as he told them, and ending up with "and after parade my name is Joe."

All the same I was afraid at one time they were not taking him seriously enough and that I might have cause to regret my choice but his seven years as a regular stood to him and once he got used to certain minor changes that had taken place in drill and instruction in the half dozen years he had been out of the army, he impressed them by his efficiency and knowledge which he imparted in a pleasant Irish way which commanded a willing response at all times.

Eames' last station with his old regiment had been Cairo

and it was said he had a knowledge of its more mysterious underworld that was the envy of the other men.

Like so many of his race, drink figured largely in his relaxations but it never showed on duty and I was accustomed in the King Country to men who had a periodical burst of it and were good enduring workers thereafter for six months on end, who could show the way to their teetotal brethren whom at that time I was too often ready to distrust, until they had proved themselves.

Corporal Joseph Eames would develop pulmonary tuberculosis and return to New Zealand in July 1915. He was declared medically unfit for military service and discharged. He died of his illness in Auckland Hospital on June 4, 1919.

At the end of January, the New Zealand Infantry Brigade, Spencer included, was sent to Ismailia to join 30,000 troops resisting a 25,000 Turkish force backed up with eight artillery batteries that had crossed the Sinai Desert, determined to take Suez Canal and hopeful that the Muslim population of Egypt would rise up in revolt against the British.

The Turks were poorly equipped; their arrival had been long expected with newspapers daily reporting their progress over the desert although it was uncertain what their chief objective would be. As it happened they moved to assembly areas just east of Ismailia.

"We ought to have all the trumps in our hands," said the military correspondent of the London *Times*, "but we must not forget that the Turks fight with courage. Military people with great traditions must not be despised."

The Turkish force, many of them ethnic Arabs, were routed, suffering 2000 casualties — another bitter defeat to add to a recent loss at Jenihos. Most of the action involved Indian troops but a platoon from the Nelson company of the NZ Infantry Brigade was the first of the Allied forces to engage the Turks.

One New Zealander lost his life in this action. Spencer referred to the Suez action only in passing:

On leave, we met many officers in the train back and forwards to Cairo. As far as one may make friends with an officer senior to oneself serving in another regiment, I had a good one in Athelston Moore now in command of the Otago battalion, and his attractive young wife who had been reared in his regiment, the Dublin Fusiliers. Both were Irish and full of fun. He was older than I by about five years with a wealth of experience in the South African war. He wore the DSO freely given to subalterns who saw fighting then. He was good about answering questions. There had been criticism on the Canal about colonial troops opening fire too soon. To my query as to when one should do it, he told me, "Never open fire until you see something to fire at."

Lt-Colonel Moore would be criticised after the Otagos suffered heavily on May 4. He would be wounded on Chunuk Bair, on August 8, 1915.

We were all getting weary of the everlasting training. This weariness was noticeable in shortness of temper, and in the case of certain old hands, sent them to the bottle. Corporal Eames was a case in point.

His work was a pleasure to watch, his manners always good, but his weaknesses were native Irish, added to the temptations of Cairo which from his former service he knew from the inside far too well.

After leaving Ismailliah [sic] he got very depressed saying, "Here we are, doing squad drill, miles behind the front. It is what I always said you never see anything but regulars in the front line. You'll see, we'll all be doing guard duty on the lines of communication till we go back to New Zealand. Colonials are never used in the real fighting."

He did not say this to me but to his cronies, especially old regulars like himself but younger men would get worried as to our prospects and question me about it. I would reassure them; but I also felt an impatience which I must not betray to the men, or allow me to influence in any way.

A notable field day was one in which our battalion supported by a field artillery battery carried out an attack against a position of trenches in which man-sized targets were set and the gunners and ourselves fired live ammunition.

As we marched out, we could see for miles in the clear morning air. This exercise was the first of its kind by New Zealand troops and many staff officers were on the ground to see it. Away in the distance we saw, or thought we saw, a group of ladies on horseback. These had no doubt been warned not to come near and they kept discreetly to the right flank well over a mile away.

"Lady Godley is there boys," said a man in the ranks.

"Come to see the sights?" said another.

"She'll want to encore the bloody show I suppose," suggested one.

"Oh! How nice! Make them run again, Alec," the first one said mimicking a female voice which was lost in a gust of laughter.

They were stepping at ease and at such times officers discreetly affect not to hear much of what is said and by the time the joke reached the end of the column no doubt it was stated as fact.

That it would be related as one in later years no one ever thought at the time, but so history is made.

This I do know, that no lady was within shrieking distance of us during that day and it could not have happened as General Godley was riding amidst the troops where he could best observe, whilst operations were proceeding and for an hour afterwards remained with General Birdwood and ourselves when the criticism, which always followed such exercises was being delivered. So whilst the idea was humorous, no real soldier could possibly believe such a preposterous story was true.

Unknown to Spencer and the New Zealanders, the chances of seeing action in the Dardanelles looked more likely by the day. On January 2 the Russian commander in chief, the Grand Duke Nicholas, had sent a telegram to the British via their ambassador in Petrograd stating they were hard pressed by the Turks and hoped a demonstration could be made against them.

The British assured the Russians a demonstration would be made although Field Marshal Lord Kitchener, the Secretary of State for War and main figure in the War Council which ran British operations, was not enthusiastic. His urgent priority was the defence of Britain. Troops could not be spared from the Western Front. In time, however, he agreed with Churchill that a stand-alone naval attack was worth a try. Everyone fell into line.

The naval attack was made by out of date battleships on February 19. British and French warships bombarded Turkish forts in the now much more stoutly defended Dardanelles Straits. New Zealand newspapers received reports that the bombardments were successful prompting one provincial editorial writer, no admirer of Turkey, to have his say on March 11 reflecting an opinion prevalent in New Zealand:

> "The Turkish public must by this time be disillusioned by any hope of profit from their alliance with Germany and must bitterly regret the crass stupidity of their leaders in embarking upon such a disastrous adventure as that alliance has proved.
>
> "Only a miracle can now save the Ottoman Empire from annihilation and there is little likelihood of such a happening. The allegedly impregnable gateway to the Turkish capital is crumbling to pieces under the Allied naval guns and to complete her downfall the Allies are concentrating a powerful force for a land invasion.

It would be foolish to suppose the Turks will be easily conquered. There is much difficult and dangerous work to be completed before Constantinople is reached.

"The Turkish Army is not to be despised. On paper there are 700,000 men under arms. The Turks do not lack courage but no troops can fight if they are not properly fed. Although field guns, ammunition and rifles have been pouring in from Krupps through Roumania, Germany has no surplus food to dispose of. Whatever happens Turkey is doomed to disappear from Europe as a Power of any consequence and she deserves no other fate.

"She has never been anything but an agent of destruction. She has shown remarkable aptitude for the slaughter of Armenians by the hundreds of thousands. In all these years she has shown no signs either of accomplishment or progress. She has no literature worth speaking of, no statesmen, no true poets — no pretensions whatever to greatness.

"If she is turned out of Constantinople tomorrow she will leave few traces of her 450 years occupation except a few mosques with their minarets and the latticed windows from behind which the lymphatic and grossly ignorant mothers of degenerate sons look out upon the Bosphorous. Unwept, unhonoured and unsung will she go." (*Ashburton Guardian*, March 11, 1915)

Contrary to what many believed, the bombardments had not been successful. In London, Lieutenant General Birdwood, commander of the ANZAC Corps having travelled from the Dardanelles, informed Kitchener it was unlikely the navy could do the job on their own. And so, after having initially rejected the proposal, on March 10 Kitchener agreed to let the British 29th Division go to Egypt.

Two days later he appointed General Sir Ian Hamilton, as Commander-in-Chief of the vast Allied force, the Mediterranean Expeditionary Force, gathering in Egypt although at this stage it was

Sir Ian Hamilton

not known what the military operations would entail.

Hamilton, the same Hamilton who visited New Zealand as Inspector General of Overseas Forces, would comment later that at the time he was appointed his knowledge of the Dardanelles was nil, of the Turks nil and of the strength of his forces next to nil.

In the space of a mere two weeks the Mediterranean Expeditionary Force of 75,000 men had to be put together.

On March 18, the Allies made what would be one final all-out naval effort to smash through the Straits into the Sea of Marmara. Three of their battleships were sunk, two others crippled and a battle cruiser damaged; 700 seamen lost their lives to the Turks 44. At first the navy wanted to continue but on March 23, the Allied fleet commander, John de Robeck, advised London the mine menace in the straits was worse than expected. The decision was made to ask the army to lead the attack on the peninsula. But much was against them. Time had been lost allowing the Turks to bolster their defences and the Allied force had many deficiencies with perhaps the worst being a chronic shortage of artillery shells.

Britain was producing a miserable 22,000 shells a day to Germany and Austria's 250,000. And as preparations were hastily made, many of the military high command knew that the decision to proceed with the Gallipoli campaign was at variance with expert advice given in a paper prepared by General Staff at the War Office just over eight years before. The paper stated:

"The successful conclusion of a military enterprise directed against the Gallipoli peninsula must hinge upon the ability of the fleet not only to dominate the Turkish defences with gun fire, and crush their field troops during that period of helplessness which exists while an army is in active process of disembarkation, but also to cover the advance of the troops once ashore until they could gain a firm foothold, and establish themselves upon the high ground in rear of the coast defences of the Dardanelles.

"However brilliant as a combination of war, and however fruitful in its consequences such an operation would be, were it crowned with success, the General Staff, in view of the risks involved, are not prepared to recommend its being attempted." (Dardanelles Commission final report p.84)

In spite of this Hamilton plugged on. His Mediterranean Expeditionary Force would comprise five divisions:

the 29th Division (17,649 men) formed from 11 regular infantry battalions and one Scottish territorial battalion;

the Australian and New Zealand Anzac Corps (30,638), still early in training with uncertainties as to how it would perform and not having done any divisional exercises or combined arms training;

the Royal Naval Division (10,007), composed of marines and sailors for whom there was no room on ships and who were poorly resourced with artillery;

and the French Corps Expeditionnaire D'Orient (16,762) which combined Senegalese, Zouave and regular troops who had also not trained together as a division.

Since January, the Turks had been preparing defences on the peninsula but now moved with greater haste improving fortifications and road networks. They were conducting intensive combined artillery-infantry exercises and practising counter-attacks designed to drive any invaders into the sea. They had been humiliated in the Caucasus and Suez Canal – which raised British confidence to perhaps unrealistic levels – but the reality was the Turks were shaping as a formidable defending force.

On March 26, the German who had come to Turkey on a military mission the year before, General Liman von Sanders, was appointed to command the Dardanelles defences. Unlike Hamilton, von Sanders had the possibility of large reinforcements should they be required. He identified three possible areas where the Allies could land on the peninsula – Cape Helles, Gaba Tepe and Bulair.

Because of the uncertainty, von Sanders decided to have the shoreline lightly defended. A company of 200 men was stationed at each beach but with divisions in reserve not far away, ready to be quickly brought in to counter-attack wherever a landing was made. He split his force of 60,000 to cover the three possibilities. To Troy, on the Asiatic coast which he thought the most vulnerable, he sent the 11th and third divisions; the 9th and 19th went to Cape Helles and Gaba Tepe; and the fifth and seventh to Bulair.

Meanwhile, on March 30, eighteen days after being appointed by Kitchener, Hamilton was in Egypt where he inspected his Australia and New Zealand Army Corps.

Spencer was among the thousands of soldiers who lined up.

# Final review

The last review in Egypt, for many of us the last occasion we would march past was held for Sir Ian Hamilton who we now heard had arrived to take command of a large army in the Middle East of which we were to form a part for what purpose we knew not; but it enhanced our keenness, many of us had been reviewed by him in New Zealand less than a year before and were thrilled to be serving under such a leader.

A bugle note brought us all to attention and we sloped arms.

Sir Ian Hamilton galloped on to the ground in front of us with a large staff on horseback and came to a halt. A bugle note again and we presented arms together to order; the officers saluting with their swords, of course we could not see the flash of thousands of bayonets behind us whilst the massed bands played the national Anthem.

Back to the carry came the swords of the officers, as the rifles returned to the slope and we looked straight ahead so saw little of the general and his staff as they rode slowly along our lines. But we gained the impression of a slim, keen man on a thoroughbred horse, several other generals Birdwood and Godley amongst them and the bright uniforms of certain allied officers. From flank to flank they rode taking quite a long time to see all they wanted and then they rode off to take post at the saluting base. We ordered arms. The massed bands struck up. The march past commenced.

We stood on our ground with time to watch before our own turn to go by should come and there passed before our eyes one of the glories of the world that will never be seen again.

To the tune of Garryowen advanced the leading squadron of the Australian Light Horse regiment in line. They came at a walk; but the horses themselves seemed to pick up their feet more daintily to the music with heads held high, ears cocked forward tossing manes and long swishing tails, the well fed and carefully groomed animals came on in perfect formation, many straining at the bridle and snatching at the bit yet easily controlled by their tall and limber riders who sat immoveable in the saddle, their rifles at the carry, butt end on right thigh as they turned all heads and eyes to the right, on the command, as they approached the saluting base. The hats turned up at the left side with a bunch of emu feathers gave a devil may care picturesqueness, the bandoliers and accoutrements indicated the fighting power.

The review took place in the full heat of the day with windblown dust being the worst the New Zealanders faced but Spencer gives no indication.

He does not mention either that on Good Friday, April 2, New Zealanders joined Australian and some British troops rioting in the Wazza, the brothel district of Cairo, venting their anger against prostitutes and brothel keepers for past grievances. Crowds watched about 5000 rioters smashing up the brothels and setting bonfires. Military police shot and wounded several men. Spencer's Waikato company had a new commander and more serious business was at hand.

Our pageantry was over; also our hardest work. Rumour was rife. We were going somewhere; but where?

Our old Major Rastrick who had never been with us after the first day in Egypt, was now finally retired from the command of the [Waikato] company. He had been a likeable old man but quite useless.

Alderman took command. This was a blow to McDonald, who, brigade recognized, had born [sic] the burden and heat of the day so far. He drowned his sorrows in Cairo the evening of the announcement and it was rather pathetic to see him marching afoot in full pack at the rear of the company where for months he had ridden at the head of it.

Alderman was somewhat of a genius in training officers in tactics. He always listened patiently to their ideas and thereby encouraged men to think for themselves. He looked the born soldier he was. Unfortunately he had a share of human weaknesses. Bacchus and Venus demanding some attention, and for those inclined that way, Cairo offered the opportunity. Nevertheless he took hold of the company at once.

Alderman, 40, had been born in Hobart and a regular soldier in Australia.

He was admired at first sight and the men liked him, as did we officers. Knowing his weaknesses, whilst I gathered he did not consider his penchant for the fair to be one, he would abstain from drink altogether for lengthy periods. This was embarrassing for those living with him who did not see why they should deny their own moderate tastes.

At this time though he was in one of his relaxed moods which meant that under the bed he kept a bottle of whiskey from which he oft replenished his tin cup. He was generous with it, to whoever was there, and consequently I had my share but after having had one I would decline a second if offered too soon, or altogether if near bed time. At one time he asked me.

"Why won't you have another? Don't you like it?"

"Very much thank you sir," said I, "but I don't find too much of does me any good."

"Really now," replied he, "I don't find it does me any harm," and promptly had another.

It rather worried me. I was never an abstainer and enjoyed the hilarity of a reunion but not when there was serious work to be considered.

We heard he came back from Cairo in the early hours one morning and coming through the horselines, gave the transport picket drinks from a bottle he was carrying. It certainly damaged his standing in the eyes of the men of the company. They thought it demeaning in an officer to let himself down in this way amongst his men of the rank and file.

Major Rastrick had been staying in an expensive hotel at the expense of the New Zealand government. Spencer said Rastrick had never got over the shock of having to bivouack in the desert. Given the choice of continuing service or returning to New Zealand, Rastrick chose the latter.

Major Alderman, later Lt-Colonel, would be wounded on April 25, and later awarded the Order of St Michael and St George for his service at the Dardanelles. Spencer:

With a move in view, the staff had a certain amount of tidying up to do. Storage of surplus kit had to be arranged, staffs for depots organized, reinforcements provided for. Our third draft of these had joined us from New Zealand. Our ranks were full to overflowing and we had to reduce our numbers to a uniform standard.

Corporal Eames was lost to me at this time. He had gone absent without leave and been arrested but with his service he was released with the approval of brigade staff. Hang me if he did not do it again! This time he was under arrest to await court martial. I hoped he would be able to clear himself as he was one of those intelligent Irishmen who had the confidence of his section and we all liked him.

So I went to see brigade. The brigade major listened patiently to my story. I said, "As I believe we are soon to engage the enemy, I would like to take the section leaders with me, that I have had all along. Corporal Eames is one of them and he is a very good man."

Major Temperley, without a flicker of a smile said, "he must be."

"Yes sir," said I, "He is. No-one has trained his section better."

"Yes, he must be a very good man, from what you say. A man who overstays his leave and because of his former service, is released from arrest without penalty and then goes and gets drunk and does exactly the same thing again is not reliable. No, Westmacott, this time I could not recommend that he return to duty."

I could not but see the justice of this somewhat sarcastic reply and had to accept the position without further protest. It was because we were staffed by men like Temperley that we became the fine brigade we were.

With a guard of 20 men I was sent over to the VD camp beside that of the 4th Australian brigade at Heliopolis and to embark the men there at Alexandria next day. We had five posts, one on each side of the camp and one at the entrance. One, whom I had known well in New Zealand, was among them [VD men]. I greeted him and told him I was sorry to see him there. Usually correct in his address, he replied more for the amusement of those standing by, than for me, in bravado with a humorous remark, but I felt for him and for myself too. One always dislikes having to enforce any restraint on an old friend.

How we packed them all into a troopship for Malta at

the end of a tram journey to Alexandria is described in a letter I wrote my father at the time I think.

About this time 445 New Zealand soldiers were hospitalised for venereal disease; 206 cases were shipped to Malta.

There were few farewells to be made in Cairo. The cosmopolitan women we had danced with at the Casino were to most of us only associates of the hour though in one or two cases officers married women of dubious antecedents to put it kindly.

The large English colony had their own concerns and would have found it difficult to know where to begin about entertaining on a large scale from the vast mass of officers unless they brought letters of introduction. The officers of the 16th all had ties in New Zealand, with one exception, that we felt precluded any lasting notions of romance. So had made no friendships worth retaining once the drum should beat for our departure.

The exception was young Stuart Baddeley. There was a house near Zeitoun station occupied by a family of the effendi or official Egyptian class. The father, a Turk we were told, was interned but this did not prevent the mother entertaining several officers at times.

There were two daughters aged about 16 and 17, both as pretty as such girls often are at that age. I had become aware of them on our departure for the Suez Canal earlier, when they came to see us entrain, and the younger, very lovely, shed a tear, that I told was for Baddeley.

He was a heart whole boy, not prone to dalliance and I later took the opportunity to give some fatherly advice about being discreet. He assured me it was only a passing friendship.

Towards the end he and I dined together in Helmiah and about 10 o'clock we paid our bill and started on the short walk of about a mile to camp when, having gone a few paces he said he would bid me goodnight as he was going to visit some friends.

I had already seen the result, in another friend of mine, of letting a light affair become serious and tried to restrain him, pointing out that it was unusual to go visiting at that hour. He suggested he was a particular friend. I said that from what I had heard the family had a number.

Asked who, I said, "Price for one," and he replied, "If he tries any of his funny business he has me to deal with!" [Captain Athol Price would be wounded April 25, 1915].

"Well, if that is how you feel about it, I suppose I shall soon have to congratulate you. Let me know when you are writing to tell your family about her.

"Oh! Nothing like that," said he. "It is only a passing friendship."

"You won't be writing to her when we go from here?"

"Of course not," he replied, and so we parted for the night and I heard no more about it whilst we were in Egypt having plenty of work to attend to. So had he, or so I thought. For next day but one came the order to move.

# Leaving

---

The move was made on April 10.

The first two companies 3rd Auckland, 15th North Auckland entrained first with half the transport in the afternoon, the colonel and HQ going with them. The rest were to follow at intervals.

We, the 6th Hauraki and 16th Waikato under Major Stuckey after an early meal, followed. I was entraining officer for these companies.

Major Frederick Stuckey, 36, like Plugge, a teacher at King's College, Auckland, would die of wounds on April 25, 1915.

Major Stuckey

As we pulled out we were cheered by the many troops who came to see our departure. These were chiefly men of the NZ mounted brigade who once again were very worried that there was no sign of any orders for them to move. [They would land at Gallipoli on May 12.] They had not been with us on the canal and now some talked of jumping the train and joining the infantry. Their turn was to come.

One of the last things I noted was Baddeley's little

girlfriend in tears on the platform. I felt we were only getting away just in time for him. Now I feel a pity for her and wonder what became of her.

Travelling through the night we found ourselves at daylight crossing the delta and watched the fellahin already commencing work in their well-tended cultivations.

I wondered if they thought about us and why train after train of troops was going down to the sea.

We ran on to the wharf. There were ships all round it, mostly occupied by French troops including a battalion of the Foreign Legion. Our ship was the German prize *Lutzow* and we were kept waiting with arms piled because her cargo was being loaded into her hatches for the lower hold and the decks were obstructed. It was not advisable to move troops on them till all was clear. McDonald had preceded me on board. We passed the time trying out our French on the sergeant of the guard of the Foreign Legion close to us.

Soon, being told the hold we were to occupy, I climbed down the hatch and found it was only entered by a single steel ladder, the rungs of which were fastened to the side of the hatch. The company Sergeant Major Hobbs was with me. Together we paced the length fore and aft about a 100 feet and the breadth about 50 feet. We saw that without bunks or furniture of any kind we could just pack the company in. There they were to live, eat and sleep until we left the ship. There was just room for all.

We sailed next day. Ships packed with troops were all round us, many being Imperial soldiers of the 29th Division, soon to become world famous. Some cheered us and our men replied "Be goin' Cairo choom?" under the impression that all Englishmen spoke with Lancashire accents, though some came from Scotland, Hampshire and Ireland.

A launch full of females singing, "It's a long way to

Tippararee" [sic] came out to see the last of us and were hardly noticed.

"They have seen enough of those," said Alderman.

"Women no longer excite them. They are real men now."

By sundown we were well out to sea. Everyone was in high spirits. Though some were still sceptical whether we would at last see real fighting. We were moving towards it and glad if we had seen the last of the sands of Egypt.

On board were General Godley and his staff, half of First Canterbury with Colonel Macbean Stewart and their battalion headquarters and our own battalion.

Allen, Baddeley and I shared a cabin. McDonald and Peake another, Peake, had no liking for McDonald. We three were glad to be together. The general and all officers messed in the saloon. Our food was plain; but good.

Lieutenant John Peake, a farmer, would be wounded on April 25, 1915.

The sergeants said they were well fed. The men had tinned meat, bread at first, pickles, jam, butter and biscuits with plenty of tea. Cooking much for such large numbers was impossible but there were no complaints.

Of course we officers visited the men's deck frequently to see all was well but there was little to do. Everyone was well behaved and physically fit. Our concern was to keep them so if they were to remain long in the ship as exercise was difficult.

This fitness combined with cramped quarters and idleness led to short tempers and fights. There were three in which blood was drawn in our company, one between Philson and Maughan Barnet [sic]. I only saw the after effects, notably a black eye for Philson.

Expressing my regret that two men who were known friends should fall out, they said generously "It had to come sir."

"I hope you are good friends again," said I and, "The very best, sir," was the reply.

I never knew the cause but I saw the beginning of another when the men around me below decks started flocking towards two big men who had commenced pounding each other just as I passed through. I stopped them and asked the cause.

Private Philson

"I told him not to kick my pack," said one, "and he told me to go and — myself," said the other.

"Well, that is not a nice thing to say," was my reply.

"But we are going to fight a real enemy any time now. So do shake hands and try to forget it."

Both Private Wilmot Philson, 29, a farmer of Te Kuiti, and Private Maughan Barnett, 21, would be killed in action on April 25, 1915.

Private Barnett

There were lectures and talks in the saloon after dinner, General Godley presiding. The Honourable Aubrey Herbert, who was a Turkish interpreter on the general's staff gave one. He was a most interesting man who had been an attache in Turkey, was a Member of Parliament for a Somerset division, had joined the Irish Guards and been at Mons.

One night he told us his experiences in the retreat from Mons where he was wounded, captured by the Germans and being left by the Germans released when our army advanced again. He has described all this in a book *Mons, Anzac and Kut by an MP.*

Herbert's other talk was by General Godley's order, about Turkey and the Turks. As he warmed to his subject he told us what fine fellows the Anatolian Turks were. How they were farmers who readily made good soldiers of great endurance under any privations and that when the fighting was over they returned to farming as easily. By the time he had finished one had quite a friendly feeling for such people. The general felt that this must not be allowed to be a lasting one and got up when Herbert had finished and very nicely pointed out what we knew of Turkish shortcomings ending up, "The Turkish soldier is capable of great cruelty, isn't he Herbert?"

"Oh, yes sir," said poor Herbert dutifully.

"And whilst I have no intention to detract from the very interesting talk that Herbert has given us, I must warn everyone that we are here to fight the Turk and beat him and that anyone falling alive into his hands will have a very poor chance of surviving."

We had at this time stories of atrocious Turkish behaviour to wounded men and all felt we must die fighting rather than yield to our enemies.

The *Lutzow* was a German prize, one of many interned in neutral ports early in the war. Egypt's neutrality did not really exist in fact as the government relied normally on British protection and our people therefore took all the German ships in the ports. Who or what *Lutzow* was we did not know. Baddeley who had once belonged to a liedertafel gave the line of a song, 'We are *Lutzow*'s riders, ahunting we will go.' But knew no more than that. It gave us all a great satisfaction to know we were travelling in German ships even if we were a bit crowded.

The first stage of our voyage was uneventful and the weather calm. A fine looking battleship passed us that we took to be the Queen Elizabeth. Her deliberate approach gave great confidence to all who watched her and noted her turrets and immense guns. Little we know. She was called HMS Tiger and was an imitation of that ship. There were a number of these 'dummy' battleships sent to sea to deceive the enemy at that time.

It was interesting being in the same ship with so many people from whom we had hitherto been separated by regimental barriers. Major 'Jacky' Hughes and Tahu Rhodes were on the staff.

Major Hughes was a veteran of the Anglo-Boer War and would later command the Canterbury battalion. Rhodes was Godley's aide-de-comp.

Colonel Macbean Stewart, a fine soldier to look at, an impartial disciplinarian and a born soldier was in command of 1st Canterbury, Critchley Salmonson, Munster Fusiliers, was his adjutant, Gresson with one of their companies, a captain, John Hill and Cliff Barclay subalterns. John Hill had been in the York and Lancasters. Cliff was the only son of Dr Barclay of Waimate and had been at Waitaki Boys' High School.

Also I found Harry Kitson whom I had known from childhood was a sergeant in that regiment. It was a good one.

Salmonson would be awarded the DSO for his actions on April 25 and the night of May 2/3, 1915. Gresson, a law clerk, later a judge and knighted, would be badly wounded on the Daisy Patch, May 8, 1915. John Hill, a Ceylon tea planter from London, would be shot through the mouth on April 25, 1915. Cliff Barclay, 22, a stock agent and son of a Waimate doctor serving with the Royal Medical Corps, would be killed in action on April 25, 1915. Kitson was with headquarters staff.

After two days at sea we found ourselves passing through the boom into Mudros harbour [on the Greek island of

Lemnos] soon after breakfast. It was a vast sheet of water land-locked by pleasant green hills. At anchor lay English, French and Russian warships and troopships of all allied nations. As we passed each ship there were cheers from them and our own men.

More than 200 ships were assembling at Lemnos ready to land at Gallipoli.

We proceeded well up the harbour and dropped anchor close to two troopships moored together with two battalions of the 29th division on board.

Already we had a great respect for these troops of the 29th. Everyone who had seen them said they were superb. The division were nearly all regulars. They had been composed of battalions drawn from isolated stations where they had been relieved by territorials, sent home to England and trained together in the most up to date tactics based on lessons learned in France. Their average age was about 25 years. All were seasoned troops, acclimatized to European conditions by this last winter in England. They were burning with resentment at having been withheld from the battlefields of France, animated, both officers and men by the best traditions of the service and a martial ardour to do or die. We felt it a privilege to serve alongside such regiments. They were the last regular units of the old army. After them all divisions were either territorials or new army.

Inside the boom all shipping was safe lying at anchor. We had never seen such an armada before. The green island looked a paradise after the sands of Egypt though the hills were treeless. As usual I was allotted a boat.

We commenced at once to practice landing operations. These consisted of parading the companies of infantry in full kit and going ashore in turn, packed in boats as close as the men could sit, their rifles between their knees. We would land, extend along the shore, advance to the nearest hill top and take up a fire position, and when satisfied everyone was ready to fight, pile arms and allow the men to roll in the long cool grass which grew up to ankle height. In this way we would spend two or three pleasant hours until our turn to re-embark and go back into the crowded ships.

# Soul searchings

Naturally many of us, probably all, though most never spoke of it, had soul searchings at times, about how we would behave under heavy fire with men being killed and wounded around us. I believed that if I allowed my imagination too much rein, I would feel it too much to the impairment of my efficiency but that if I concentrated on my work, my mind would be free of disquieting thoughts.

Baddeley had once remarked on the startling noise

Lieutenant Baddeley

bullets made, misses as well as hits, as they went overhead when we were in the marking butts during musketry [training]. McDonald in his emphatic, not to say rude way, told him that if he gave thought to such things he would be no good as an officer.

That was one way of dealing with possible misgivings. As we had leisure on board ship I thought it better to talk such things over. Where anyone had reassuring counsel it was far more likely to help, if we shared it.

Noting Baddeley reading the Bible in the cabin I said that as I had neglected to so long when safe and well, I was diffident about doing it now on the eve of battle.

Allen indignantly said I was wrong in this and I felt I was. I did not say that I had first read that point of view in Sir Evelyn Wood's *Midshipman to Field Marshal*. I got so many of my ideas from such personal records and the talk of veterans who had seen older wars.

Lieutenant Allen

Baddeley, Allen and myself were closer at this time sharing a cabin as we did, than for some time past, when, though sharing their feelings about McDonald, I suppressed them. We were not a happy family inasmuch as McDonald and Peake hated each other too, yet had to share a cabin.

Baddeley was a strong character enough to know he would rise above fear. His fear was the common one, that he might show fear in his bearing. I said it was easy to overcome this. He said "How? I have never seen you in any kind of funk?"

I told him I had.

"When?" he asked.

"When I took the boat out at Albany and I thought the sea would swamp us. I longed to be back on board ship."

"But half of us were seasick and you sat in the stern smoking a cigar."

"It was because I was so frightened that I smoked the cigar. I learning during the strike in Auckland when I thought things were going to happen, to put a pipe in my mouth, even if I had not time to smoke it, it had a soothing effect, especially when waiting.

He looked incredulous but I am sure noted what I said.

Fears, concerns, worries were inevitable for soldiers never under fire before now about to encounter this greatest of tests. Each soldier viewed the prospect in their own way and in most cases did their best to suppress and hide their feelings.

A private in the Canterbury Battalion, Cecil Malthus, also with Spencer on the *Lutzow*, wrote a letter to his future wife on April 3 in which he said they were not so keen on getting to the front. "I know we are supposed to pretend we are but now that our first enthusiasm is over, I think most of us are quite willing to keep our skins whole." (Letters, Canterbury Public Library, Christchurch)

Spencer wrote, however, that to him no-one seemed unduly worried.

Reverend Fielden Taylor

On the Sunday we practised landing as usual and the Reverend Fielden Taylor, chaplain of the Canterburys in our ship, took advantage of the occasion to hold an open air service. It was a fine day and he went off with the first tow early and standing on a grassy mound said a prayer and gave a short service. The men having piled arms lay on the grass around him, listening attentively — it was entirely voluntary — and they came and went — he certainly had a quiet magnetism and held his congregation but it was more than that.

Everyone there knew in a vague sort of way that many of us would presently die, and whilst no-one seemed unduly depressed at the prospect, we were in solemn mood and ready to pay heed to the preacher's words which were something like this: "As you have lived, so will you die and it does not very much matter," uttered in quiet conversational tones which we all found strangely satisfying, even comforting. Perhaps they are one and the same.

As each tow of boats came ashore, newcomers approached and sat down whilst the first to arrive were recalled for the return to the ships.

He was there when I arrived and continuing in the afternoon when I left. I believe with prayer and exhortation he went on all day. A Sermon on the Mount it seemed. Comparing notes after, I do not believe any of us forgot it.

It had been planned that the landing take place on April 23, but strong winds forced a delay. It was put back to Sunday April 25.

April 23 was out last day in harbour. [The *Lutzow* moved.] Next day we remained anchored outside the boom. The mail came aboard from our loved ones. We were issued with cigarettes which surprised us as they had been forbidden before. No-one was allowed away from ship except a party who buried Lance Corporal Bigwood who had died in the night. He was a good looking Englishman who had come out, spending lavishly, a large income from home after the South African War in which he had served. Younger than he, I had envied him when I saw him in Christchurch years before.

Women adored him there and in Australia where he had married lovely little Carrie Moore of Merry Widow fame. Now I was his officer. [Captain] Price went through his belongings. It seemed pathetic that he had deferred his allotment of three shillings a day to Carrie who was making over two thousand a year on the stage. Price made up a parcel of things to send to her. He consulted me about some letters from another woman. Bigwood was hopeless in that way. I said destroy them and he did.

Corporal Bigwood died of pneumonia at Lemnos, April 22, 1915. He had a brother, Sergeant Wilfred Bigwood, also serving in the Auckland Infantry. Both came from Birmingham, England. Spencer:

Baddeley got a letter from Egypt which made him furious with himself. "I am a brute," he said, "A real brute."

The explanation was that heeding my advice not to get

involved, he had not written to his little girl at Zeitoun and now he received a letter from her reproaching him for it. She knew he could have got a letter to her as Price had written! Of course she did not want to hear from him. In view of what was so soon to happen to him, I hope he wrote a penitent letter then and there to catch the next mail back as he never saw her again.

Officers came aboard from other ships to decide final details, whether the men were to carry firewood was one. Moore the Dublin Fusilier commanding 1st Otago was one of these officers. I asked him to my cabin afterwards. He came and had a yarn. He tried to maintain his usual light facetiousness but he decided after that he was not feeling cheerful. He had been in Buller's army in Natal, knew what stiff fighting was and whilst making light of it outwardly, was worried at the magnitude of the task before us.

All communication with the shore having now ceased, we got our detailed orders and studied them with the aid of the maps. It seemed rather a dispersion of force. We were to land at widely different points but the Australian and New Zealand Army Corps had one objective and Brigadier General MacLagan's third Australian brigade were to land first at daybreak and push forward to a defined line to cover the landing of the rest of us.

It was impressed on us that on our part of the field, the main feature was a commanding hill numbered on the map 971, the Turkish name being Chunuk Bair.[1] If we got astray in the advance, we could do no wrong if we located it and made for it. To capture it would be the first objective of the corps after making good our landing. The New Zealand Infantry Brigade — ourselves — were to land after the Australians, go into reserve, and advance through

1 Hill 971 was not Chunuk Bair; 971 was named for its height (971 ft); Chunuk Bair was 860 ft.

the Australians the following day. We were disappointed not to lead but one has to do what one is told.

The Australian and New Zealand landing would be one of two main attacks. The second major attack would be made by the 29th Division at Cape Helles on the southern tip of the peninsula, at two beaches. One of these was codenamed V beach, where an old collier the River Clyde packed with 2100 men would run ashore, the other would be at W beach. The navy would bombard the Cape Helles coast beforehand.

Three other less intensive landings would be made on Cape Helles at S, X and Y beaches. The Royal Naval Division would make a diversion at Bulair to draw in the Turkish forces there — New Zealander Lieutenant Commander Bernard Freyberg, future commander of the 2nd NZEF and Governor General, would swim ashore and set off flares giving

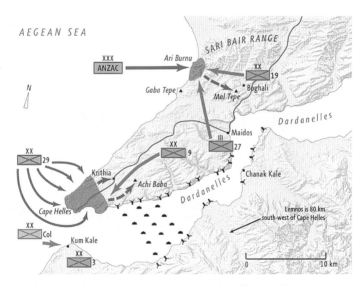

A map showing the Anzac landing and the other Allied attacks on the peninsula. The Anzacs' objective was to land at Ari Burnu (now Anzac) and take Hill 971 and Male Tepe. The 29th Division was to land on five beaches on the southern tip of the peninsula with their objective being Achi Baba. The French were to make a diversionary landing at Kum Kale. The Ottoman Fifth Army's 19th, 27th and 9th divisions are marked by boxes 19, 9 and 27.

(Courtesy NZhistory.net.nz)

the impression something was happening. In another diversionary action the French would land a brigade on the Asiatic side at Kum Kale and Yeni Shehr.

The two chief players were the Australian and New Zealand Infantry Corps and the 29th Division. After taking Hill 971 and at Cape Helles, a hill, Achi Baba (718ft), which dominated the southern peninsula, these two main forces would consolidate and then advance to take the Kilidbahr Plateau. On board the *Lutzow* it was calm before the storm. Spencer felt a coolness that had arisen between him and his Waikato company commander, Alderman, was now a thing of the past.

We had a quiet afternoon. Colonel Chaytor invited me to his cabin where we had a long intimate talk.

Our batmen had to draw lots as to who was to remain aboard. Each company left one to keep the officers' kits. Fish, my batman was the unlucky one with us. He never quite forgave me; McDonald left them all with a grievance by exempting Alderman's man and his own from this lottery.

Colonel Edward Chaytor was a veteran of the Anglo-Boer War and a friend of Spencer's father. He was senior personnel/logistics planner for Godley and would command the NZ Mounted Rifles in Sinai and Palestine.

That afternoon we communicated the gist of our orders to our men who of course were very interested and if there were any faint hearts they were not noticeable. We had parades in full marching order to see everyone was in possession of all that was ordered. As none of them had any other possessions in the ship this left the hold empty of everything. The men were in great spirits.

The evening was a quiet one. Some of us gathered in Alderman's cabin. The padre had brought some liquor aboard and we had a drink but there was no hilarity. This padre had jumped the ship. He had been our chaplain but was ordered to remain in Egypt and he was sent ashore and returned there before we sailed. I had been very outspoken about him saying that if I were wounded and dying he was not to come near me as I would not go into the next world in a proper frame of mind. I would welcome Father Dore.

Chaplain Captain Patrick Dore, a Roman Catholic chaplain, would be wounded in action at Aghyl Dere, August 22, 1915, and die during an operation in connection with the wound, July 15, 1918.

I had qualms about drinking liquor he had paid for but to refuse would have been conspicuous. The conversation naturally turned on the task before us. Someone voiced a feeling all must have had about the possibility of failure and its consequences. It was no use thinking of that. I said, "We are not going to fail. We shall get ashore all right, carry out our orders and be in Constantinople in a month."

There was a noticeable silence before Alderman said, "He is right. He has his prejudices but he is a soldier and there is nothing the matter with his outlook on war."

It was a great pleasure that Alderman should speak of me like that, not because he was my company commander, and I had anything to expect from him, for my views were over independent for my subordinate rank, and whilst I was very ambitious, I felt that any position I might attain to would entirely depend on my work when facing the enemy; but because he had started in Auckland by reporting very well upon me to higher command and made me feel I had a friend who would trust me.

But when at Ismailia the quartermaster had boasted to me that he had, with a party of his men, picked up a barrel of beer, belonging to someone else, on Cairo platform which he had brought down for battalion headquarters mess and any other of our officers who cared to send a dixie for some and invited me to do so I told him that if I heard of anyone stealing I would put him up, whoever he might be and as Alderman was then on HQ mess and had some of the beer, he was not pleased when the remark was repeated to him and told Macdonald, who told me. "I am disappointed in Westmacott. I thought him a man of the world." So now I felt that we would go into battle with complete confidence in each other.

We knew a landing under fire had not been carried out since Sir Ralph Abercrombie landed in Egypt in 1800 and in those days there were no machine guns or long range rifles.

So to bed early with the idea we were to be under way about 1am.

We slept soundly.

# April 25, 1915

Dawn had not come when we awoke to find our ship steaming along on a calm sea. I had hardly turned over to go to sleep again when the rumble of guns made me jump out of my bunk and the two others joined me at the porthole.

They were the guns at Cape Helles where the 29th Division must by now be going ashore. Day was just breaking. There was a slight mist along the shore. Save for flashes from ships' guns we could see nothing in the half light. It was nice and cool with the promise of a glorious day. It was a little after 4am. I said, "We may not rest so comfortably tonight. Let us go to sleep again," and we did very quickly. My words were prophetic. Before another night both my friends were dead.

First awake in the cabin I looked at my two companions, as with innocent faces, they lay in their bunks, childlike in their slumber. Soon awake we were up and dressed at 7am. And went to Holy Communion with Fielden Taylor in the saloon. I noted among others Colonel Braithwaite, [British soldier seconded to NZ forces] Price [recently confirmed], Baddeley and a number of the NCOs and men. We bowed our heads as we waited on our knees and followed the words "in remembrance that Christ died for thee."

Waiting to land: This illustration depicts Australians on their ships
— it could easily be New Zealanders.

Breakfast was at 8am. We visited our men. They were all happy and well fed too, though their fare was plain. I asked Sergeant Major Hobbs how the sergeants had been fed. He told me they had no complaints. They had not had much cooked food for all the way across, but "plenty of 'am, sir, very good 'am." Those were the last words we had off duty together.

We went on the top deck. The ship lay at anchor several miles off shore which was clear to see a rugged coastline. There were ships all round us, a magnificent sight with bright sunlight shining upon a calm blue sea and clear sky. The high cliffs of Gaba Tepe afterwards called ANZAC were straight ahead.

Yes, and there they were, real shells bursting like puffs of cotton wool against the clear blue sky at the summit of the cliffs. Pictures had always shown a simultaneous flash and smoke. We noted that the flash came first leaving the smoke afterwards. Interesting. Someone was getting it under those bursts at that very moment.

To right and left of us, a mile or so away in each case, our warships lay close in shore pounding away at the enemy's position and between us and the beach, at the foot of the cliffs, a stream of destroyers, picket boats and lighters crowded with men plied their way back and forth ceaselessly.

As we watched, at about 9am a heavy roll of musketry from a ridge to the left of where the troops were landing grew to a roar and then died away to a few occasional dropping shots.

Colonel Chaytor's eye caught mine. His shoulders rolled with pleasure. His eye lit up with the lust of battle as he heard it and he nodded his head at me as if to say, "Now we shan't be long."

News from the shore commenced to circulate among the decks. We were told that the leading troops were safely landed but there had been considerable opposition which had been overcome with heavy loss to the enemy. Like good soldiers nobody enlarged upon our own.

A destroyer came alongside and from her bridge an unshaven young officer looking very untidy hailed us through a megaphone to say, "Colonel MacLagan has taken three Krupp guns." The news ran like wildfire through the ship and there were cheers from all the decks. Colonel MacLagen commanded the third Australian brigade. He was an imperial officer, one of the original Duntroon instructors. Mac Weir who had been under him there said, "Good old Mac. Trust him to do it."

The colonel [Plugge] and battalion headquarters Major Harrowell and Captain Price had gone ashore with the leading troops. Third Auckland under Dawson and Sixth Hauraki under Stuckey went next with the New Zealand Engineers. The officers with 3rd Auckland were Captain Fraser, Lieutenants McFarlane, Woolley, West and Carpenter and Company Sergeant Major Page.

6th Hauraki Company were Major Stuckey, Captain Courtenay Sinel, Lieutenants Algie, Morpeth, Flower and Dodson, Company Sergeant Major Robertson.

15th North Auckland Major Bayly, Captain Bartlett, Lieutenants MacLelland, Weir, Screaton and Steadman, Company Sergeant Major Partridge.

16th Waikato Major Alderman, Captain McDonald, Lieutenants Peake, Westmacott, Baddeley, Allen, Company Sergeant Major Hobbs. Lieutenant [Andrew] Frater [died of wounds April 30, 1915] was the machine gun officer and Morgan was with the transport animals in another ship. Captain Graham was quartermaster and Hatt the regimental quartermaster sergeant.

Morgan was the earlier mentioned rather casual Lieutenant Harry Morgan. Adherence to military routine did not necessarily create a brave soldier — Morgan would distinguish himself at Gallipoli. After the landing he would crawl from the trenches night after night to bring in wounded. On May 8 while trying to rescue a fellow officer he would be shot through the head by a sniper and killed.

All fully equipped we now went below to the troop decks and inspected our men who had been fallen in and were awaiting us. All ranks were in caps like the British infantry. This applied to the Australians too being a corps order. We had noted with disapproval that when 3rd Auckland went ashore a few men wore hats, but their discipline was slack.

Once again we checked over the equipment, satisfying ourselves that each man's water bottle was full. It had to be water, we would have liked cold tea. When we had seen the three days extra rations, the men fastened breast pockets and the usual 150 in their pouches and closed them too.

I carried the silver cigar case, presented me by my troop in the strike the previous year with the Huia feather and greenstone Kereihi had given me, and some letters in it. These I wrapped up in a black silk scarf and put in one breast pocket, my small pocket bible in the other. Most men carried the latter.

We gave the order "Charge magazines," in went 10 rounds and the cut-offs were closed.[1] I loaded my RIC revolver and there was a short silence so I said, "We are about to go into action. We are all ready and remember that if anyone is hurt no one is to leave his place to take him to the rear. That applies to me as well as all the rest of you. The stretcher bearers are there to help the wounded. Remember also that I will allow no man to open fire unless we see something to fire at."

The leading platoon now began to climb upon deck and the others in turn filed after them.

On deck we formed up in our platoons in close order and waited. I had 56 other ranks, the company strength being 223. Sergeant Bennett asked my permission to fall out. I gave it.

Biscuit tins full of water were placed at intervals on the deck and our orders were to drink all we could of this as our water bottles were not to be used without permission, probably not until night, and the water we drank now would abate our thirst until then.

We doubted this, or rather I did, in view of past experience but we did as we were told.

As we were doing this Sergeant Bennett who had resumed his place again asked to fall out.

I said, "Certainly sergeant but is there anything the matter?"

He looked confused and said, "No sir."

I said, "Well, you will soon be back?"

He said he would and he was there before we moved.

---

1 They carried ·303 short magazine Lee Enfield rifles which were capable of firing 15 rounds a minute.

Lieutenant Barclay

Young Cliff Barclay passed me going to his platoon of 2nd Canterbury further along the deck. He said, "We are going ashore in a minute. The lighters are coming alongside."

We wished each other good luck.

It was shortly after 10am. Alderman said a few words to the whole company.

"We are going ashore now, but I do not think anyone is going to be killed today!"

At which there were roars of sceptic laughter from his listeners. They were all in such high spirits that we felt it

This photograph appeared in New Zealand publications at the time of the campaign captioned "New Zealand soldiers being towed by a destroyer to the hostile shores of the Dardanelles."

was glorious to lead such men who now obeyed the order to file to the right and down the ladder.

Alderman and some of ours filled the first lighter. My platoon were in the second and two platoons of the Canterbury regiment, whose Colonel Macbean Stewart and his battalion headquarters also came and took their places forward. Critchley Salmonson, their adjutant and I sat near them on the port side, our legs hanging over the water.

Jack Anderson of divisional HQ who was being left onboard and with Von Kettle [Lieutenant Dudley Kettle HQ NZED] looking disconsolately down at us over the rail, waved to me and I waved back. We were quiet enough. There was no talking at this stage. A destroyer was to take us in. The tow rope tightened. We were under way.

Never while I live shall I forget the grandeur of the scene. In front was the coast, rugged and steep, but with easy country to the right front and beyond Achi-Baba with huge 15 inch shells bursting on it from HMS *Queen Elizabeth*. The fire was deliberate. Minutes would pass between each shot which seemed to scrape up the mountainside, bursting on top like a volcano throwing tons of earth high into the air. It was a cheering sight to us but terrifying to the enemy.

To our right, close in shore, stood a balloon ship with an observation balloon glistening high in the sun. Right and left, broadside on to the shore were the battleships steaming slowly and firing at the Turkish positions in crashing salvoes which went booming and echoing among the hills. About halfway to shore we passed on the left, HMS ship with General Birdwood on the bridge. He smiled shyly down at us after looking through his glasses but was unnoticed by the majority. Cotton wool puffs over the ridges ahead showed where the Australians were holding the ground won and being shelled.

A lighter was towed past us filled with wounded lying quietly for the most part, one or two here and there sitting up, or propped on an elbow to look at us. I think they made us feel rather envious. They had been under fire. We had not. We felt they were one up on us. They were soon behind us and we were looking forward.

Our men sat smoking for the most part, their rifles between their knees. They were crowded as close as they could sit and quite imperturbable, gazing towards the shore.

Colonel Stewart sat near me on the small deck near the bows. Similarly placed astern Regimental Sergeant Major Mooney [Sgt Major Robert Mooney, HQ Auckland Infantry, Liverpool born, killed in action August 7, 1915] and Hobbs, the latter puffing away at his pipe, sat amongst a group of sergeants. I thought what fine soldiers they looked and then of their wives and families, Mooney with his baby daughter, Hobbs 56 years old with five children and not a gray hair in his head, a veteran of South Africa

A sailor shows the strain steering one of the boats packed with soldiers towards the Gallipoli shore. The *Lutzow* is in the background.

in the Scots Guards. I do not suppose when he came to New Zealand he ever expected to see fighting again. He looked placid enough as he approached his last battle.

With the two ropes tightening and sagging we continued towards the shore. At bow and stern a naval rating standing erect and for some reason each was supposed to be disguised as a colonial soldier, this simply seemed to mean he was more untidy than usual and wore an Australian slouch hat, obtained where I know not. These were there to keep the towed lighters running straight.

We approached the shore and the beach became visible. Lines of wounded lay in the sand. Officers and men were moving about. A party of Australians were building a jetty by throwing stones into the water. A man stark naked was bathing in the sea. A stream of wounded was straggling down from the hills. Parties of men were at work making tracks up the cliffs. From the ridges beyond came the sound of fighting.

The beach seemed sheltered and very quiet. Our destroyer ran close up and turned to the right running parallel with the shore. Our sailors cast us all loose and we drifted on, closing in on the beach under our own way. The leading lighter approached the jetty of stones aforementioned and the men prepared to go ashore when ordered.

A handsome staff officer with fair hair and moustache, clad in light breeches and puttees, a helmet on his head, no jacket and his sleeves rolled up the elbow, came down the edge of the water and shouted, "Come out of the boats, New Zealanders."

We continued sitting and gazed at him while he grew red in the face. Considering that he should call for the officer in charge of us and say, "Get your men out of the boats."

Instead, after repeating himself, he got sarcastic and shouted, "Are the New Zealanders afraid of wetting their feet?"

At that I saw Salmonson raise himself with his hands and we both jumped into the sea together, going into the water right up to our waists at once. The men poured over the side after us en masse, without a word from us, those further astern going right in up to their necks. Their readiness to follow us unbidden seemed magnetic. At this moment a Turkish shell burst overhead.

We waded ashore, shook ourselves and met Captain Thoms of the NZ Staff Corps who directed us to the left.

The water squelching out of our boots and clothes as we walked, we straggled along to the forming up point in a small gully, picking our way past the wounded on the ground. A certain amount of confusion was apparent. There were packs, rifles and other articles of equipment all over the beach and at one point a number of packs had been built up to form a barricade, rather an ineffective one I fear.

The first soldiers from the Auckland battalion land at Gallipoli.

Our men still carried miscellaneous things besides their rifles, the machine guns four, and the tins of water from the ship. Rounding a spit of land from the slope of the hill, on the way to the gully where we were to form up, we came under heavy rifle fire; but it was not serious for I saw no one hit though I stood there till all my men had passed.

As I waited there Colonel Braithwaite came up to me and pointing at the company in the lead as he did so, said, "Is that your number one company?" and I replied "that is the third Auckland company, sir." After which he asked in his usual tone of irascible irritation, "Is it Dawson's company?" "Yes sir," said I.

"Then it is your number one company," he said emphatically as if I were a damn fool. I held my tongue though I was irritated as it had always been impressed upon us that we were to adhere to territorial designations, and reflected I would have been slanged in any case, whatever I called it. He went forward hurriedly and left me.

The battalion had formed in the gully in close column of platoons, our own company being the last to come up, was still telling off sections. A.C. Cowdray [sic; Pte Albert Cowdrey, killed in action, April 25, 1915] said to me, "If the section commander is not present sir, should not the next man form up the section?"

I said "Yes. You do it," and he obeyed smartly.

I never saw Sergeant Bennett again but heard he was wounded in the hand on the beach, losing it afterwards.

We moved off, the 3rd Auckland leading as usual. But presently the whole battalion sagged to a halt. I saw the colonel [Plugge] move towards Alderman and soon we were all turned about placing the Waikato company in the lead.

What next? thought I.

Alderman called to me, "Westmacott, take your platoon into the lead and stay there."

While moving through Baddeley's platoon Colonel Braithwaite bustled up to Colonel Plugge and said loudly, "Reinforce the first Australians on the left. Reinforce the first Australians on the left!"

When Plugge turned towards me and said, "Yes, that's it. Westmacott reinforce the first Australians on the left."

It was the first and only order I heard my colonel give that day and it was not his fault either. The regiment was very confused and bunched owing to Dawson's company having run into an unclimbable cliff and being turned about towards the rest of us.

No parade ground formation seemed possible here and Braithwaite's close presence with his excitability made me eager to move away from him.

I called to my platoon to follow as they were and led the way up, by what seemed the shortest route along the hillside. At a later day I would have been more deliberate in my movements but I had been ordered to take the lead and did not wish to show any sign of hesitancy when going under fire for the first time.

I came quickly to where a party of Australian engineers were making a zig zag track to the top and almost immediately cut off an angle of it making a run up. I was followed by some of my more active men and from where I was above them helped others by taking their rifles by the muzzle and pulling them up till six men were with me, when I saw it was too steep for most of them and told the others to follow the track already well defined and half formed.

The men at work were steadily improving this thoroughfare to the top, picks were breaking down the hard clay and shovels were sending it flying. Our men were pressing up, crowding the workers, but it was the only way and we had to get on.

Also, wounded Australians were coming down here

and there. We had not the heart to stop them, but they delayed us a little. This perhaps had an advantage as some of the men were getting a bit blown.

Alderman joined me at one of these checks, quite out of breath and relieved to pause for a moment. Someone tried to pass a box of Australian ammunition forward past us, it did not fit our long rifles and Alderman said, "Don't worry about that lad, until we get forward."

I said, "But I think we ought to pass it on, sir. The Australians must have their ammunition."

I had more wind than most after climbing Rangitoto for over four years and the box went on from hand to hand ahead of us.

Only about a minute's spell was indulged in here, until our men began to bunch up behind us and our next move upward carried us to the hilltop where we found the track entered a Turkish trench which followed the contour of the cliff from which it stood back three or four feet and was fairly straight for the most part.

It was a good field of fire out to sea but obviously any troops who succeeded in reaching the beach were almost immediately in dead ground, unless the defenders climbed out to hang over the cliff edge.

This perhaps accounted for our initial success and progress on reaching the shore. It was a little puzzling as we had expected from our orders to find ourselves on fairly flat ground at the beach level. It was only afterwards that we learned the landing had been made in the dark at the wrong place. No general would have dared to launch troops at those cliffs. It was a lucky accident, however, for the Turks were well dug in and waiting for us at the obvious place.

"Keep going Westmacott," were Alderman's last words to me so I now went like smoke along the trench which bore to our left, which, I gathered, from what had been said on the forming up point, was the direction in which we would find the First Australians, from whom I could expect to get a clear idea of what was required of us.

However, soon several of my men behind called me, "Mr Westmacott, a message."

I stopped and word came.

"Halt, and let the rear close up," and I waited whilst my men crowded up, there was only room for single file, the trench being about three foot wide. Everyone was hot and red faced with the pace at which we had climbed and come on. They wiped their foreheads and smiled when I caught their eyes. Another message arrived, repeated from man to man, with care, as they had been taught, "All packs off."

We complied.

I told everyone to put his pack in rear of the trench. I placed mine under a bush, specially noting its position behind an angle, and never saw it again. Whilst doing this a company of Australians in single file who had reached the top, just here by another track, passed over our heads towards the firing line, which was across a wide valley on the inland side of the hill top where we were.

We exchanged greetings with them till the word came for us to advance again, and now I came on several dead Turks, both on top and in the trench. We had to walk on the latter. In that hot sun their presence was just noticeable though they had only died soon after dawn, but not yet unpleasantly so.

Now I came to the end of the trench and my first problem. It opened down a hillside. To the left was a steep and scrubby slope with no track. To move along it would be a slow progress. To the right there was a track, obviously the enemy's entry to the trench which went on down an open razor back and was under fire for some distance.

If we took the left hand hillside it was so steep it would

be climbing along it slowly under fire all the way. The bullets were smacking on the bare clay of the razor back almost at my feet as I paused there.

Each course before me seemed unpleasant but I could not remain undercover of the trench and continue the work I was there to do. I took the quick decision to go down the hill and up the bottom of the valley to the left, as affording the best cover to our men. Waiting till they had closed up I called to them to follow and led the way down.

It was time to double. I saw no use in waiting to see them out of the trench or any kind of heroics and no one lost any time about following just as fast as I went.

On our right we passed a Turkish tent covered with branches of scrub. The Australians had been there before us and I did not stay to examine it. We never paused until we reached the valley bottom where I thought we were in dead ground again, and halted whilst the men came down. The ground was damp but there was no stream.

On the reverse slope of the opposite ridge where the track we had followed went upwards, an Australian was standing with rifle and bayonet. In answer to my enquiry he pointed to a spade stuck in the ground beside him and told me he had been posted there to prevent anyone touching it in case it was a booby trap.

"Beware mines," he said knowingly.

The company were clustering behind me and I called for number 15 platoon men to join me, which those present did.

Here John Hill, of the 2nd South Canterbury came down to me. He said his platoon was with us in the rear having somehow lost touch with their battalion and followed us forward. He was a little troubled as to his position and asked the question, "If an officer loses his CO he joins himself on to the nearest senior officer does he not?"

Knowing the answer to be yes, but seeking moral support, for I found he had three platoons with him under subaltern officers, Cliff Barclay being one and no senior. On my reassuring him he asked, "Who is your senior officer?"

I told him "Major Alderman. You could not follow a better."

He reported to him. They came on with us and were of the greatest assistance later. Whilst standing here a sniper got on to us both and we stood back under what cover there was. Private Arthur Clarke of Otorohanga said, "There is the man firing at us sir. I'll shoot him."

He pointed his rifle up the hill but as I could not distinguish the sniper and the Australian fighting line must be somewhere over the crest above where Clark was pointing, I was afraid of firing into their backs and told him not to. He lowered his rifle but he and others continued to watch until we moved again.

Whilst here the Australian company who had passed us on the hilltop delayed us by crossing our line of advance and ascending the opposite slope. They seemed to know what they were doing and their quiet steady progress was reassuring, had we needed it, which we did not but it is always good to feel that the men about you are quiet and purposeful.

Once they had gone on we got the men together and followed the gully up to the left. There was an occasional Australian straggler but they were cool and collected and certainly not for us to worry about I thought. We came to a group of Turks lying apparently sunning themselves on the bank at the gully bottom. A young Australian soldier stood guard over them, with rifle and bayonet. Somehow I was reminded of a fox terrier with a number of dead rats in a barn. He was wagging his tail I felt.

"What are these men doing here?" I asked.

"They're dying sir," he said delightedly.

"They have all been bayoneted and I am posted here to see they do no harm."

Pride and pleasure was in every note of his voice. The poor fellows were accepting their fate quietly enough.

Next I came on a group of about eight or nine Australians. One stepped forward, called me Spencer and proved to be Otto Strachey. [Pte Strachey, 27, 1st Battalion, Australian Imperial Force, killed in action, May 2, 1915] We shook hands. We had been at Waitaki together. The last time I had seen him was at Suva, Fiji, when *HMS New Zealand* was there two years before.

I said, "Where is your officer?"

He said, "We haven't any officer now."

"Then, come along with us," said I and he said they would like to.

In reply to my question why he was with the Australians he said he had started from Suva to enlist in New Zealand and on reaching Sydney, NSW, had feared he would be too late for it all and had joined up there. His companions seemed willing and glad to be with us. This party preceded us at first but they had with them a burly, red faced man with South African war ribbons who seemed to have more to say than any of them and kept delaying them saying, "Sit down boys. No hurry," and as they were inclined to follow his lead, I led our men past them.

By now we were in what was afterwards called 'Shrapnel Gully.' The shell fire was constant but light and too high overhead to do much harm. We kept halting frequently to let the rear come up. During one halt a shell did burst closer than usual overhead throwing some dust and twigs over us. At the whistle of it, the nearest men threw themselves against the side of the gully. My mind was too occupied to take any notice and I was caught erect but unharmed in the centre of the gully. Remembering what we had been taught I said, "It is too late now to take cover when you hear the whistle of a shell."

Private
Ned Cowdrey

E.W. Cowdray [sic; Pte Edwin 'Ned' Cowdrey] said, "It is not that, sir. We were just taking cover while halted," and I replied, "Quite right. I am sorry," and so I was for the implied rebuke for doing a sensible thing. However, I was reminded of the incident long after and told it had a good moral effect.

Since leaving the forming up point at the foot of the spur on the beach we had seen no staff officer. At first we had been finding our way and enquiring the direction from wounded men. For some time I had not seen any. So I waited until Alderman joined me and said, "It seems to me we should have someone in front of us sir. I think we ought now to go up this spur. I believe the First Australians are up there ahead of us but have had nothing definite to tell me so."

Alderman said, "Yes. Send up a patrol of four men. We will wait here."

"Now then," said I to the nearest, "I want four men to go up to the ridge, find out who is up there and report back to me. Who is going?"

Jack Peterson of Te Kuiti, now a lance corporal, Dick Sircomb [sic, both Sircombe, 25, a farmer, and Petersen, 19, would be killed later in the day] of Otorohanga, Arthur and Ned Cowdray[1] all sprang forward.

"No! I will not let both Cowdrays go together. Come along another man!"

I spoke quickly and with emphasis and another man McKinnon immediately took Arthur Cowdray's place.

From then on the latter remained close to me, covering my back wherever I moved. Gillanders [Lance Corporal Alexander Gillanders, 34, killed in action later in day,

---

1 Cowdrey's enlistment papers give his name as Albert, not Arthur.

native of Inverness, Scotland] was another man who offered for this but he also being now a corporal in charge of a section, I kept back.

Off went the patrol, opened out in scout formation and disappeared on to the top. We waited, watching the short knee high scrub with which the hill tops were covered until Dick Sircomb [sic] reported back, "The First Australians are on the ridge between two and three hundred yards along sir."

Lance Corporal
Gillanders

"Right," said I. "Come along," and led the way up to him.

The men came straggling up in what might be called file, but was really stringing along as the slope was steep and bare though not very high, being near the head of the gully. Once on the crest, a few yards along the track which was well defined, I noted to the left a shallow depression which grew gradually to a gully towards the cliff and the sea. This in itself was like a wide trench.

I ordered the men to file along it, take three paces extension and lie down on the gently sloping bank in the enemy's direction so that they could use their rifles if need be. When they had numbered off and lain down I found I had 28 men.

I divided them into two sections under Corporal Grant on the right and Gillanders on the left. The Australian seven prolonged the line to our left and when I strolled along to them found they had conformed to our formation. I said they would act under me and asked if they understood things. They smiled and looked willing and a likely looking man of the natural leader type answered that they were glad to act with us. I did not see the man I had noticed before, with the SA medal ribbons at this stage and fancied he had fallen out.

It was quiet here and the depression about eight foot

deep at the bottom, the sides gently sloping to the ridge in front and behind, and the artillery fire was going over us. I strolled along to about the centre of my line and said, "If you take my advice you'll have something to eat because you don't know when you'll be able to have another meal."

Several men asked, "May we have a drink of water, sir?" to which I replied, "No water may be touched till evening and then not without permission. It may have to last three days," and suiting the action to the word commenced to eat a biscuit. The men laying their rifles beside them did the same. Looking back I saw some of the company had taken the wrong spur to our right and were half way to the top but were already turning back. I could see two officers who I supposed to be Peake and Allen directing them.

The advice Spencer had given on board the *Lutzow* to Allen and Baddeley about smoking to help control fear had been adopted by Baddeley.

Baddeley now came up the track followed by his men. He had a pipe in his mouth though not a great smoker but it looked insouciant and the effect was excellent.

He formed his men up exactly as I had done in one long line close to and covering mine and they commenced opening their haversacks and bringing out biscuits.

Baddeley and I smiled at each other and spoke a few words — our last on earth together — and as we went on eating biscuits I noted his platoon were about the same strength as mine.

Alderman now arrived very much blown. I told him the situation as I knew it, which was not much and that I was giving my men a spell for some food. We all three had a small council of war.

He pointed out that the rest of the company having gone astray as we could see, would be some time coming

When this illustration appeared in New Zealand publications it stated:
"The invasion of Gallipoli: The amazing bravery and dash of the
New Zealanders and Australians in gaining a footing on Turkish soil."
The illustration bore little resemblance to the nature of the
New Zealanders' landing on April 25, 1915.

up to us, and decided that I was to go on and reinforce the
First Australians at once with my platoon.

Baddeley was to follow with us and come into line
when there was room. He himself would wait until the
rest of the company came up before supporting us. As I
left he said, "Wait a minute. Which way are you going?"
and I gave the only possible reply I thought, "Straight
along the ridge sir."

It was but a few paces to my post in front of the centre
of my platoon whence I ordered the men to put away their
food. There was a pause whilst they did up their haversacks
once more and fastened their belts.

Looking to right and left I saw everyone was ready and
looking happy and confident and turning in the direction
of the enemy waved my arm to advance and doubled up to

the ridge. Then I remembered Mooney's advice, "Do not get in front of your men, sir," and stopped till they came in line with me, which they all did with alacrity and we moved forward rapidly; but owing to the flat top of the ridge we found we were not under close range rifle fire and slowed down to quick time to keep our wind to the last possible moment.

The men were moving at the trail, I went slightly to the right, satisfied myself that my right flank guide was moving as near to the gully as possible, and then went out to the left a little where I could see the party of Australians advancing steadily in line with us. I noted they were carrying entrenching tools with them and Otto Strachey had a pick in his left hand. Good boys! I felt a glow of pride.

Also, I realized that in these movements I had again been in front of my line and supposed I should have been behind. Never mind, that would do for a later day. It was hard to hold back now and easier to observe each man's face from in front.

The hill top was covered with scrub knee high. The track which we had followed all the way up ran diagonally away from us slightly towards our left front. The gully on our right was steep but not unscaleable as we found to our cost later on.

The ridges beyond, which were held by the enemy, ran parallel with us and up towards a high hill which was on our right front, overlooking our line of advance.

On the left the country fell away precipitously down to the sea but we could not see this as our direction was carrying us each minute further away from it, leaving more space on our left flank into which, without loss of time, Baddeley advanced his number sixteen platoon.

Swish! Swish! Swish! We strode on through the scrub, each man gazing forward as he walked. One stumbled and gave a laugh as he regained his place. "It was a dead Turk," said he, and so it was and there were more of them, quite a number lying at intervals and right across the track where the First Australians had got them when we heard the heavy firing in the morning.

The bullets were cracking round us now. We were getting it on the right but there was nothing to indicate its direction. We could see no live enemy.

Steadily we moved on. Suddenly, from in front appeared an Australian officer running like a deer. "Hullo! There you are! For God's sake push on!" he shouted as he came.

I signalled my men to "Halt — Lie down" and the officer also stopped, panting. I sat down and he did too. It seemed no place to stand about. He sat there, beating the ground with his hand, his breath coming in great gasps. When he recovered a bit I said, "Now. What's the matter?"

"For God's sake push on," he replied. "They are getting hell in front and I am going back for reinforcements." This between gasps.

"All right," said I, "I am going to reinforce in a minute. Those are my orders but I want to know what to expect. Tell me all about it. What do you mean by "getting Hell?"

"Well, they have formed a firing line in front."

"Who have?"

"The First Australians, and they're getting hell."

"That's what I want to know, that the First Australians are there all right. What do you mean by Hell? Are the Turks attacking with the bayonet or what?"

"No! No! They are losing a lot of men. They have formed a firing line on the other side of the hill and are holding on. But they need reinforcements badly and I'm going to get some."

"Very well," said I, "That's all right. We shall reinforce at once. Now as you go on down this track about 100 yards you will find my company commander in a dip on your right. He is an Australian officer. Tell him what you have just told me and give him the message from me, that I am pushing straight on."

I heard afterwards that this message was never delivered.

The officer jumped up and ran on. I rose and waved my men to advance again. It was a pleasure to see the good line all were keeping with the interval named and no bunching. The platoon were moving across the track towards their right which was the directing flank still. As we marched on we began to get it, a heavy fire passing over us. I passed a man called Mullins who smiled at me saying, "This is a hot corner, sir."

"It is that Mullins," I answered delighted to find him there and in such good spirits for we had once had our doubts of Mullins.

Private Hugh John Mullins, a plumber, would be wounded in the hip on April 28, 1915. Later in the campaign he would be appointed lance corporal. In France, he would be wounded on September 1916 and promoted to lieutenant in October 1918. Two months later he suffered a nervous breakdown. After the war he was permanently hospitalised due to shellshock.

My own suppressed excitement was intense and took the form of uttering praise in lavish terms I rarely used, "Good boys! Good lads!" and ridiculously "Good little boys." The bullets were passing all round us, making a crack as loud as a rifle and seemed very close to our ears.

I marvelled we were not all hit and thought "if I can come through this, I will survive anything."

Yet in spite of talking nonsense, my head was astonishing clear. I judged it time to pause and get our bearings, so I raised my arm in the signal to halt and take cover again, which the line did, as one man.

Of course I lay down in the scrub with them. That scrub

saved many lives that day for whilst stopping no bullets, it gave cover from view.

I was able, by cautiously raising my head, to see how we lay. We were approaching a gully, our line being almost parallel to it. It was the head of the steep gully on our right which as it shallowed towards the top curved to our left towards a ridge or neck of land which connected our hill top with a higher feature overlooking us beyond.

The track which at first we had been following up and then on the hill top had crossed, curved away from us and went on over the neck apparently following the top of the cliffs along the coast which I could see from where I was. Though shallow to our left front, the slope was steeper in front.

It was no use staying where we were for we had little field of fire, though that we were under heavy enough fire ourselves, even if the crack of bullets did not convince us, was evident by the dead and wounded Australians who lay in the scrub everywhere around us. It was easy to find our way now by these bodies on the ground.

A little further forward then, must we go, to be properly effective, so I rose crouching and signalling my platoon up, crept the last few yards which brought me to the edge of the gully, whilst I had the gratification of seeing out of the corner of my eye the backs of my stout lads as they crawled forward the way we had so often practiced to a position where each could use his rifle.

They were under admirable control and obeyed like machines. We reached the edge of the gully but the situation was extremely puzzling to me for as yet I had found no officer in charge.

Where were they all?

Failing anyone to tell me anything I stood up to try and locate the enemy, very foolish I know, but lacking information one must find out things for oneself. An officer would be failing in his duty I knew if he did not seek to do this. I got up quickly and at once the fire was tremendous.

I suppose each man fired so suddenly at sight of me without taking careful aim, that all went by me. In any case I had had so many escapes I had begun to think I could not be hit. A quick glance round was enough to tell me no more than I knew before, but I had obviously been seen by the Australians in front for a voice there called impatiently to me, "Don't stop up there. The firing line's down here."

Thought was quick at such a moment. I decided there must be an officer there and the firing line being on the forward slope, must be in a trench.

I decided to go and signalled the men with an under arm wave to follow and looking to right and left long enough to see them rising to obey my order led the way down the slope.

The fire was very heavy, terrific it seemed to me. I doubled less than 20 yards jumping over dead men, and tripping over a bush fell forward into what had been the firing line of the First Australian infantry. From the time we moved for this last rush we were met by such a hail of bullets I expected each moment to be our last.

Yet it is curious I did not seem to care at all. It was all so impersonal. A. C. Cowdray who had covered my back steadily up till now, fell beside me behind the bush and having seen me fall asked, "Are you hit, sir?" and I answered, "No, thanks Cowdray. Keep your head down," for the bullets were grazing the scrub a few inches above and cutting the twigs off the bush in front of us.

Poor old First Australians! Their firing line had almost ceased to exist. Who had called out to me when we were on the ridge I shall never know. There was no trench. Lying on the forward slope without protective cover, every man there had been killed or wounded. They had fought out there unsupported rather than retire and I saw at once that the same fate awaited me and the few of my men who had got so far forward.

We could not retire of course, nor could we advance until reinforced. Nothing remained but to stay where we were and hope that something would happen to ease the pressure upon us. What could happen we weren't quite sure. We had some vague idea that the troops on our right and left might get on and force the enemy back and we had our rifles to get a bit of our own back if the enemy attacked us in front and in enfilade from the right.

Ten yards behind Spencer, Sergeant Ward, his platoon sergeant, a London born mill hand, was lying among Australians with bullets flying over his head. An Australian next to him got his rifle up to fire and just as he pulled the trigger a piece of shell struck him on the head splitting it from top to chin killing him instantly. Ward said he felt awfully frightened but his courage returned. Some Turks approached 30 yards away. A dying Australian major ordered fix bayonets and charge. Six men to Ward's right did and were killed by a machinegun just in front of them. Spencer remained where he was. Spencer:

So we lay amongst the dead and wounded Australians. One lying just in front of me made me feel ashamed that I was sheltering behind a wounded man and that I must move away but taking him by the foot I found he was already stiffening and must have been dead some hours.

These men had most of them gone down in the fusillade we had heard from the ship about nine in the morning. A warm sun had been shining on them ever since and the wounded were calling for "Water!" also "Stretcher bearers!"

A man to my left called, "Where's our bloody artillery?"

Strange the moral effect from guns! But "water!" was the worst cry. Otherwise all lay quiet. Behind us on the hill we had first ascended from the beach, was an Indian mountain battery. They would fire steadily for a few minutes and then seemed to be silenced by the weight of Turkish gunfire, whose shells seemed to be bursting right on top of them.

We thought that was the end of them but presently they would start firing again. They were only small guns but their presence was most encouraging.

And they remained in action on and off all the time.

This would have been No 26 Jacob's battery, No 7 Indian Mountain Artillery; the English officers and Indian gunners had used mules to take their small 'screw gun' up Plugge's Plateau. The battery had three 10pd guns and landed at 10.30am. The other battery, 21st Kohat, landed at 6pm having waited for lighters since 8.30am. This was the only on-land artillery support the Anzacs had throughout the day on April 25.

Apart from the ships' guns these were the only artillery support we had. The warships did their best for us but it was difficult for them because of the cliffs to observe their fire and once a very heavy shell burst just in front of us, almost too close to make us want any more.

We were supposed to put up screens to mark our positions. My platoon did not carry one but in any case were under too heavy fire for us to have done so. We were out of sight of the ships because of the cliffs above the beaches. Eric Rhodes who was gunnery officer in one of the large ships supporting us, told me they could not see us from the control stations in their highest top.

Cowdray, very tender hearted, wanted to go back for stretcher bearers and asked my permission to do so. I said "No. Stay where you are. You'll only draw fire and no stretcher bearer could come here."

"Well then, sir, may I give that poor chap a drink of water?"

"I looked at the man he pointed to. He was a fine young Australian soldier who was lying on his face. He had been shot from a flank as he advanced and lay where he fell. The bullet had entered just above the hip bone and come out on the opposite side about the same place. He had nearly bled to death. He lay in a pool of blood, which, still dripping slowly from his wounds, had congealed and formed a small pyramid on each side of him.

He had been trying to get at his water bottle and to do so had undone his belt and tried to wriggle out of his equipment. It had fallen to the right, the brace catching his left arm at the bend of the elbow. He was too weak to struggle and as he lay, with his face to the left, could do no more to help himself. But every now and then he gave a faint call for water.

Private
Albert Cowdrey

It was futile to allow Cowdray to try and help him. He might have been killed. So I forbade it but I saw I could do so without the same risk as I was nearer. Keeping my head down, I crawled to him, unfastened the bottle and put it to his lips, where he muzzled it like a baby.

I freed his hands and left him so with his mouth against it and returned to the shelter of my bush. He cannot have lived long but for many months after it comforted me, in hospital, and does today, to think, "At all events he had his drink before he died."

From the front, from the right, and now from the rear the rifle fire was coming. The last got several of us, though we did not know it at the time for a sniper lay there just on the edge of the plateau and picked us off as we showed up, one by one.

I think he had crawled out of the gully after our right flank had passed; I learned this afterwards.

Cowdray was the first to get it. He was talking to me one moment, the next his blood was pouring down his face from his forehead. He gave me a surprised stare, then quietly laid his head on his rifle on the ground in front of him and was dead. I felt his death dreadfully and do still today. I could not help talking to his body as if he still were alive, calling him poor little boy and telling him, "Never mind."

The two brothers were among the finest men I have ever known, physically and morally, bush bred, the best type of New Zealand youth, than which I know no better in the world.

This was battle, however, with both sides closing on each other and where, though each was largely invisible they were feeling their way towards the enemy.

Soldiers now appeared about 600 yards off moving inland from the sea coast. My obedient men had lain until now under all this fire without firing a shot.

Some to my left rear saw these men first and called to me, "There they are, sir! There they are! May we open fire?"

I called back, "No, don't fire. They may be our own men," as they were undistinguishable at that range from ours who, if they were there, were moving in the right direction to soon take the pressure off us, and I wished they were.

I believe them now to have been a flanking party of a larger force of Turks advancing to the hill in front of us, following the top of the cliffs and turned inland by a curve in the coast line. I got my glasses out and whilst focussing on them they disappeared behind the hill.

Raised on my elbows I continued to examine the landscape on front through the binoculars, a good pair of Zeiss which my cousin Rupert had given me, when I received a blow on my right arm close to the shoulder which turned me right over. I was now on my back and my arm completely useless. Reaching down I found something that seemed cold, fat and heavy at my left side on the ground. It was my own right hand. I was lying on my smashed right arm, though how I got there I know not. I looked at my wrist watch. The time was ten minutes past two. I reached for my pipe but could not get hold of it as it was in the right side pocket of my jacket.

Turning cautiously over on my face again, my arm fell into position. I gave some groans, and was very ashamed of them. They were concern for myself. The arm was not painful but numb. I got relief by rolling on my left side, taking hold of it and pulling it tight.

A bullet had shattered Spencer's right arm from armpit to elbow.

Suddenly, perhaps 100 yards away to our left front, a line of Turks appeared. They were only a section of about eight but there were others behind, a small party leading would be the point of an advance guard, moving in quick time and absolute silence as trained soldiers should, well extended and searching the scrub as they came on, their rifles at the ready.

They were well equipped and uniformed, wearing the Enver helmet. Like all the Turks we had seen they were of good physique, sturdy peasants, drilled fighting men. They were following the track.

I shouted, "Fix bayonets — rapid fire!" immediately reproached myself for not giving the range and remembered it was not necessary as our rifles were sighted point blank at that distance. My good sergeant Ward lying behind us, as was his place, called.

"Now then! Don't forget. Firing with the bayonet on, put the sights up 150," and I thought I ought to have said that too and felt rebuked.

Our fire ripped along the ridge and the whole of that

leading section went down in the scrub, but more were to follow. I reached for my revolver, knowing I must use my left hand with which I had schooled myself to shoot accurately but instinctively trying to rise on my right and getting no action, went face downward in the dust and got my mouth full of dirt.

I was spitting this out as I rolled on my right side, drew the revolver and turning to the front again, pushed it along the ground, determined to hold my fire till they were six feet off, aim for the stomach and get a man for every bullet.

Our men were fine shots and now, at last, they were getting their own back, the survivors of them. The fire from the ridge behind and to the left was so steady and rapid that the Turks went down like ninepins — as they came in front of the ridge — so I have written, but it is a wrong description. One moment they were moving towards us and the next collapsing into the scrub, perhaps crumpling is the better word.

The foremost ones got no nearer than 60 yards from us. They at one stage tried to rush but moved steadily on. No doubt many unwounded took cover in the scrub, as we had done, and hoped for better times but as the advance came to a standstill these began to get up and in ones and twos and run back to the ridge.

The broad flat packs on their backs made a good mark. Not a man got more than a few yards before he pitched forward on his face. Not one reached the ridge. For a few wild moments I wanted my men to continue firing until there was no sign of life in our enemy who lay visible but was soon ashamed I should feel like that. I am always sorry for wounded and prisoners but I was not then. The blue sky looked clear above me as I turned over and looked up at it. It was not until long afterwards that I learned we had met the head of the Turkish counter attack and beaten them back. But it was only a check.

There was now a lull in the firing when from the rear came the word "Retire! Retire!" Several of my men called to me, "There's the retire Sir! There's the retire!"

I was terrified at the thought. Not only did "Retire" mean to sacrifice the ground we had reached, it meant leaving all the poor boys who lay there wounded, besides the bodies of our dead friends.

To my concern it meant possibly leaving me, though I did not, as yet feel disabled. I felt how selfish I was to think of such a thing but we had been warned about false orders to retire and I felt I must stop it at once.

So I called, "No! No! Don't retire find out where the word came from."

There was nothing for it. At any cost I must get up, back to the ridge, and check any movement to the rear. When I stood up the enemy's fire reopened. It must have been hasty. I was not hit then but when I turned my back I felt everyone was firing at me. Real fear came upon me and I commenced running. Fortunately — for I might have gone — I only got about 15 yards when I was hit again close to the spine and the force of the bullet knocked me over on my face where I lay thinking I had a mortal wound for while I had felt the bullet strike me, I had not felt it make an exit and imagined it to be in my innards. I thought I did not want to die there.

As if in answer I heard Sergeant Ward's voice saying they would get me out somehow. He had seen me fall and, at risk of his life, crawled forward to me. On the other side a young Australian soldier, quite a boy crawled to me also, each kept close to the ground.

Just behind on the ridge Corporal Grant said, "I am going for stretcher bearers."

I called out, "Keep down for God's sake," but it was too late. He had risen to his knees. He was mortally wounded through the chest. He got back but died in Alexandra [sic, Alexandria].

Ward crawled to a body a couple of yards away, to get the sling of a rifle to put round me and pull me through the scrub. I said to young Australia, "For God's sake go back my boy. I'm finished and you will only get killed," to which he answered with decision, "No! I'm bloody near crying myself sir but we won't leave yer."

Ward returned. I felt he must not help me and said, "Go back sergeant. Leave me. You must take command of the platoon now."

"I beg pardon sir," said he, "It is no use talking like that but there is no platoon left."

I had not realized we were losing so heavily before but his statement was true. Meantime we had been reinforced by some of our own men who held on doggedly. So I gave up protesting and allowed myself to be assisted.

Ward put the rifle sling round my body and tried to pull me but it would not work, as my kit, chiefly the haversack and water bottle, caught up in the scrub on each side of me. We took off the equipment placing the water bottle for which I already felt the need, on my chest, also my binoculars which had been given me by Rupert and had cost money, and my revolver, taking the lanyard and strap in my teeth.

My two rescuers took me by the left arm and pulled. I kicked with my heels at each pull and seemed to go back nearly a yard at a time. I was on my back, and they on their faces, had to wriggle back after each pull.

This was good progress but I soon dropped all my kit, except my cap, which I was able to keep on. The revolver, glasses and water bottle kept rolling off however and catching in the scrub and I had them recovered, till Ward said, "Don't worry about them sir. They can be picked up later on. We are trying to get you out."

I did not want them to delay or risk their lives more than need be, so I saw the sense of the remark and left the things behind.

Progressing painfully in this way, and it took time, I thought we went about 30 yards and got well over the ridge before Ward said, "We are under cover now sir, and could get back quicker if you could walk."

I stood up and for the first time felt very faint from loss of blood. They both supported me and we soon reached the track, which was being shelled, behind the firing line where I learned that our whole company was engaged and some of the Sixth Hauraki company had also gone in on the left of us.

I tried to report to Major Alderman but we could not find him. I was afraid I was becoming rather too dependent on assistance and allowed myself to be helped along the track towards the rear.

About 100 yards along I saw Captain Courtenay [sic][1] Sinel kneeling at the head of a platoon of sixth Hauraki. His commander, Major Stuckey, was already missing by this time, having tried to lead his company along the steep hillside from the Turkish trench and no doubt died in the scrub, for his body was never found.

Sinel and the men with him were under shell fire at this point and losing heavily. I exchanged a few words with him, tried to tell him about the enemy and how our men were holding on the ridge ahead, but am afraid I was not much help to him and I learned later that I had bled so much down my jacket front and breeches that many, as they waited, were concerned about me.

I certainly was not a nice sight at this stage, my right arm hanging useless and saturated with gore. No doubt Sinel was glad to see me go, for to tell the truth I was beginning to feel a bit faint and did not notice things very clearly.

The shell fire at this stage was a thing we did notice.

---

1 Captain Courtney Sinel.

One four gun battery of the enemy had the range of that track to a yard. It fired in salvoes. There would come one burst of shrapnel 'Bang!' and then close following almost all together 'Bang! — bang! — bang!' and the bullets and fragments spread with an angry sish-sish, sish-sish through the scrub, and then there was a pause before they fired again.

At first we threw ourselves upon the ground when the first shell burst and waited for the three to follow, and when the salvo ceased would get up and move slowly on.

I was again wounded, this time by a piece of shell casing, I thought, which knocked me down, but apart from cutting my jacket and bruising me did no great harm. Then we moved into the scrub on the right, well away from the track, and it was not so bad. Had we been more experienced soldiers we would have done this earlier as tracks drew shell fire.

At this moment a man of ours, with his foot blown to pulp, came hopping out of the scrub behind us and cried out, "For God's sake. Don't leave me."

The young Australian went back saying, "Come on mate. Get on my back," and the man held on to him.

I thought I might not see the lad who had helped save my life again and wanted to know who he was and report his brave action to his officers. So I asked his name.

"Don't bother about that sir," he replied. "I know what you want it for. My name is Nip Knox. That's what it is."

Two men with the surname Knox were serving with the 1st Australian Battalion — 1969 Private John Knox, who would die in France on May 5, 1917, and 1562 Private Leopold Upton Knox, who would die of wounds, November 15, 1916, in Harefield Hospital, Middlesex, England. Spencer:

By this time I could not walk more than a few yards at

a time and only very slowly, with assistance, getting up, getting down, staggering along.

We now found ourselves over the edge of the steep slope into the gully. Someone said, "It's no good. We'll have to get a stretcher."

So they put me down on the ground where I lay very content with my eyes closed, but feeling the thirst.

As I lay there the sixteenth Australians commenced to pass me going into action along the ridge which was a reassuring sight. I might have expected our 3rd Auckland and 15th North Auckland at this stage. But they were not there, nor was battalion HQ.

Instead the 16th Australians were pushing forward in groups steadily and purposefully. I had stayed in camp with them in Egypt and knew the officer who led them, revolver in hand, and he recognized me, asking, "Where are they Westmacott?" and I could answer, "Right ahead, keep on the track and you can't go wrong."

Ward went off and presently returned with a sergeant of the Australian Medical Corps. He cut off the sleeve of my jacket and shirt and bandaged the arm.

The bullet had entered the back of it just below the shoulder, shattering the bone and tearing a great hole out the front.

The limb dangled. It was still a relief to pull it tight which I did, sitting up, and I felt it was so numb I could have had it off then and there without anaesthetic but did not think it would be necessary to amputate.

The sergeant broke some twigs off a bush close by and tied them round the wound, like a splint, I thought, but suppose it was a primitive tourniquet. For the first time it began to hurt a little as he tied it but he said it would help me if I could stand it and it was by no means unbearable.

Under a bush nearby lay a youngster in full kit on his

face. I thought he must be very badly hit, at first that he was dead. But whilst my arm was being attended I had seen him move a little so I asked my attendant now to do what he could for him.

He went and turned him over asking, "What is the matter mate?"

"Where have you got it?" and the lad said, "Oh! I'm terrible bad."

The sergeant then examined him carefully and said to me, "I cannot find anything wrong with him sir."

I told him there must be and he examined him again.

"No," he said. "There is no wound."

Nor was there. He was skulking to save his own skin and if his feelings drove him to that when his mates had gone forward, what must they [his feelings] have been as the refuse of the battle, like myself, were assisted past him to the rear? I let him lie where he was though I felt it was my duty to order him to be kicked forward, for his own sake. He was not the only one that day but they were rare. The only runner to the rear that I saw, was the Australian officer early on, and the fact was that once landed on that beach it was easier to push forward into the fight. There was nowhere to run away to.

The medical sergeant returned to me. I asked for some rum to help my thirst which was, I felt, unquenchable. He had none but gave me his water bottle full of brandy which bucked me considerably.

I now asked him to look at my body wounds which I thought were serious but they proved not as bad as I thought.

Two small shell wounds were nothing but the bullet wound which knocked me over the second time was a narrow escape, striking near the spine, it had slid round the left ribs coming out with a large exit on my left side but doing no permanent damage though I bear a couple of good scars to this day.

I now felt much more chirpy thanks, doubtless to the brandy. They took my jacket off and after emptying the pockets threw it away. I asked them to keep the buttons for me but they said we could get plenty more. I would have liked them as souvenirs. They said it was hard to carry a stretcher down the slope, could I walk to the gully bottom?

I said I would try. The sergeant took off one of my puttees, tied it round my neck and slinging my arm in it, they stood me up. To the bottom of the gully was about 50 feet I should think and almost precipitous. I could find foothold like a goat at that time so used was I to steep country and I reached the bottom in about two spurts, my escort being harder put to it to keep their feet than I.

Collapsing on the soft sand I lay there on my back whilst the sergeant went for a stretcher. Presently a wounded Hauraki man appeared and sat on the bank beside me. The lower part of his face and jaw were shattered. His eyes looked out of a bloody bandage tied all round his head. Of course he could not speak.

Presently, drawing his bayonet, he motioned me to watch while he wrote with the pointing the sand of the bank, "Lieut. Morpeth wounded half an hour ago."

I felt very pleased for up to that time I thought I was the only officer of our regiment hit and felt rather a fool in consequence.

The sergeant returned with the stretcher. I had a last drink of brandy and when I returned his water bottle he said, "Do you know sir that you have drunk all my brandy?"

I did feel ashamed of this. I do now. Two men lifted me on a stretcher. I was carried up the winding pathway and I do not remember much about it except that we were very slow and sniped at. But the enemy being a good way off on the far side of the gully beyond the Australian firing line no one was hit.

At one point they had to put the stretcher down and take cover while the bullets smacked the side of the bank over their heads. But it did not worry me for the sergeant's brandy made me feel optimistic and we soon moved on again.

The journey was a dangerous one. They carried Spencer down a valley where they rested. The next part meant climbing another valley to the beach and safety. It would require moving 500 yards in full view of the Turks.

The medical sergeant stayed behind as two soldiers, one an Australian, helped Ward carry Spencer through this difficult section. Before starting Ward took off all his equipment, apart from ammunition and water bottles, leaving them in the care of the medical sergeant. They set out. Sergeant Ward: "After an awfully hard and tiring journey, with many times having to drop to the ground to avoid the sniping from the Turks, we eventually got Mr Westmacott down to the beach."

Ward's great efforts had saved Spencer's life:

It was dusk as we reached the top of the hill and the landing place was below us. Just over the crest was a small dressing station where they examined my wounds. I asked for brandy and got it.

They sent me on down the path. I lost my cap here which I valued and had clung to all the way. Down the slope which was crowded with little parties of troops, men were still cutting tracks whilst others were making little shelters to sleep in. Others again were boiling water in their mess tins, heedless of the turmoil the smoke from countless little fires ascending in thin wisps into the still air.

Seawards lay the ships, black hulks upon the still water, while boats of all kinds swirled in with troops who were still disembarking, all along the shore, and picking their way among the wounded who still lay in rows upon the sand. Overhead still burst the shells, whilst ever and anon came the roll of rifle fire from the hills inland.

On reaching the beach a surgeon came to my stretcher and asked me about myself. I told him how the sergeant had tied my arm up with twigs in case it needed further attention.

On looking at it the surgeon said, "It is a rough job but quite a good one. He has stopped the bleeding."

He examined my other wounds quickly and told me I ought to be all right until under cover when I could be properly attended to, "I tell you what I will do," he went on, "I'll put you on a lighter straight away."

There was one lying close to us, on the beach, being filled at the moment with wounded. I was hoisted in, two blankets placed over me and what with the day's excitements not forgetting the brandy, was soon fast asleep.

Some time later I awoke. Darkness was complete by now but I could see boats on the water and the forms of people moving about on the beach, a light here and there where a surgeon attended his work, and the spark of little fires on the hillside, whilst now and again a shell would burst and illuminate its immediate surroundings in a momentary red glow.

Everything was quiet and business-like.

The lighter was towed on to the shore, her nose resting on the sandy beach. A seaman of the Royal Navy was sitting in the bow close to me, and another dimly visible at the stern. The intervening space was crowded with wounded on stretchers and there was an undercurrent of grumbling which I realized from the occasional remarks of one or two lying close to me, though the quiet patience of the men, many of whom were suffering, and none crying out, made me proud to be among them. They bore their wounds in silence.

Our seaman at the bow was sitting there smoking philosophically and discussing every day affairs with one in a lighter lying close to us. I soon got sick of this so I said, "What are we waiting here for? Why don't we push off to a hospital ship?"

Our seaman replied in tones of weariness, "Well sir, we can't you see. Both hospital ships have gone to Alexandria. They were full at midday."

"But," said I, "It will take four or five days to get there and back."

"Yes sir," said the seaman, "That is just what it will do," in a tone apparently quite pleased at my mental grasp of the situation.

"But," I said I, "You can't stay here all night." Everyone was listening in the boat now, so I determined to have local public opinion on my side.

"There are wounded men in the boat, and it is going to do them no good lying in the cold like this."

"Yairs," said a wounded Australian lifting up his voice, "and I'm shot through the bloody belly. It is no good to me stopping out here all night, either."

"There you are," I continued my oration once more, "Listen to that man. He's shot through the stomach. Just you get us taken on board the first ship you come to, whether it is a hospital ship or no. At least we'll be under cover."

"Well sir," answered the seaman. "We can't get a tow out."

"Nonsense!" said I. "Call out to the nearest destroyer or picket boat. Say you are full of wounded and there is an officer here who wants you to be towed out to the nearest ship."

This was done. Our seaman only needed someone to speak with the voice of authority and after an interval we were made fast to a picket boat and under way.

The first ship we came to would not have us, had no doctor on board, they said, and we were towed slowly on, feeling very forlorn, wandering round like a lost dog in the night, but we had more luck at the next ship. We went slowly past her anchor cable and stopped.

"Who are you?" they hailed us.

"Wounded men from the shore. There is no hospital ship. Can you take them aboard?" "Who are you?" the young naval man in charge of our towing craft spoke for us.

*"City of Benares* with First Australian Field Ambulance, waiting to land," was the reply.

"Wait a minute till we see the captain."

The interval did not seem long as we drifted on the still dark water, before we were hailed again by the same cheery voice.

"All right. Send 'em up."

It took some time to bring us alongside the ladder. Then it was decided to hoist up one at a time, and nets and men were sent down, stepping on to the lighter close to me.

I said, "Hoist up that chap with the wound in the stomach."

But a man lent over me with a lantern and said, "No! We'll hoist up this Briton with the smashed shoulder first," so my stretcher was placed upon a net and presently I hung between sea and sky till being lowered on the deck.

I was lifted and carried along and finally placed on a table just inside the door of the mess deck of His Majesty's Transport *City of Benares* and my wounded companions of the lighter, to the number of about 70, were carried in after me and placed upon the other tables.

A pleasant faced medical officer visited me. We all received beef tea. I asked if my batman Fish whose name was written down, could be signalled for from the *Lutzow* to come over with my kit, and was soon fast asleep.

One of the doctors said he visited me with the morphia syringe but I did not require it. In any case I had a superstitious fear of morphia or any kind of drugs and dreaded becoming an addict.

So ended the most glorious day of my life.

# Review

While the day was over for Spencer, ashore the situation for those still fighting was desperate. Late in the evening, Birdwood dictated a message to Godley which was conveyed to Hamilton on the *Queen Elizabeth*:

> Both my divisional generals and brigadiers have represented to me that they fear their men are thoroughly demoralised by shrapnel fire to which they have been subjected all day after exhaustion and gallant work in morning. Numbers have dribbled back from firing line and cannot be collected in this difficult country. Even New Zealand Brigade which has been only recently engaged lost heavily and is to some extent demoralised. If troops are subjected to shell fire again tomorrow morning there is likely to be a fiasco as I have no fresh troops with which to replace those in the firing line. I know my representation is most serious but if we are to re-embark it must be done at once.

Hamilton was handed the message at midnight. He replied:

> Your news is indeed serious. But there is nothing for it but to dig yourselves right in and stick it out. PS. You have got through the difficult business, now you only have to dig, dig, dig until you are safe. Ian H.

The Anzacs dug in.

Lying on the mess deck table Spencer soon felt deeply saddened "losing so many men in our first show." His batman Fish came over from the *Lutzow* which had taken on 400 wounded. What remained of the Auckland battalion would be withdrawn from the line next day. When the man most responsible for saving Spencer's life, Sergeant Ward, called the roll of the Waikato company only 27 were there to answer out of six officers and 223 men who had landed.

Ward would record in his diary that 64 survivors eventually assembled, 122 had been killed or wounded with 37 missing believed killed. Of the six Waikato company officers Allen and Baddeley were dead and the remainder wounded.

Eventually Spencer would piece together the fate of his men and the Auckland battalion in that one afternoon's action. Fish would bring him some of the details.

Fish said "Major Alderman is wounded sir. His arm is broken. Captain McDonald is on board the *Lutzow*, shot through the lungs. Mr Allen has been killed. They had to fall back a little they reckon and he was lying there on his back.

"Sergeant [Herbert H.] Smith closed his eyes before they left him but he was smiling and looked quite happy. Yes, Sergeant Smith was wounded too and a lot more. They don't seem to know what happened to a lot of them."

Peake was wounded and lost his arm. Baddeley was missing. He and his platoon got further forward on the seaward slope than we did, being in dead ground there until the counter attack overwhelmed them and he and an Australian officer there who survived had discussed what they were to do.

Sergeant Major Hobbs was missing. Neither was ever found. Of our four platoon sergeants Pearce [sic], Warwick and Young were killed.

The wounded were got on board ship if able to help

themselves and some were carried once they had reached some kind of cover.

Corporal Gillanders, modest and brave, was shot through the head whilst passing an order. Young Jack Peterson took over the section and was killed too. Edward Cowdray and Ned Turner were hit close together, the first through the chest and thigh, the second by a bullet smashing both legs.

They lay awhile and thought what to do. Cowdray was for trying to crawl back but Turner, with a touch of native fatalism, said he would wait for stretcher bearers. They both did so for what seemed a long time until Cowdray said he would make the attempt.

Ned Turner wished him luck and he reached safety to recover in hospital and be wounded twice again in France each time getting two bullets through him. Ned Turner died where he lay. The wounded in the ships were taken to Alexandria, Malta and some to England.

Sergeant Warwick

The list of those from Spencer's company who died included:

Lieutenants Allen and Baddeley;

Sergeant Major Hobbs, Sergeant Pearse who Spencer had trouble with during the march on New Year's Day, Sergeant Warwick, 21, Sergeant Young, 23, Sergeant Burbush;

Corporal Leonard Grimvale, Corporal Fred Haycock, 21, Corporal Donald Lane;

Lance Corporal Gillanders, 34, Lance Corporal Petersen, 19;

Private Eades

Private Bond

Private Couston

Private Lawrence

Private Cowdrey, Private Joseph Eades, 20, Private Maughan Barnett, Private Augustine Bond, 25, Private Malcolm Charteris, 28, Private George Couston, 26, Private Ernest Cox, 22, Private John Bowman, 24, Private John Dove, Private William Hartland, 27, Private Thomas Hayward, 26, Private Eric Lawrence, Private Alexander Martin, 20, Private Samuel Meekan, 22, Private David Onion, Private Francis Paine, Private Robert Passmore, 32, Private James Paterson, Private William Pearmain, 44, Private Wilmot Philson, 29, Private Henry Proctor, 23, Private Herbert Reading, Private Richard Sircombe, 25, Private John Small, Private Charles Talbot, 36, Private Carl Thoresen, 24, Private Ned Turner, Private Herbert Watson.

Private Carl Sittauer, 22, would die of his wounds on April 27; Private Christopher Boyce, 22, who was hit on a lighter coming in would die in Egypt on May 3.

The troops on board the *Lutzow* had borne the brunt of the fighting by New Zealanders. Having landed first the Auckland battalion suffered the worst with 100 killed and 220 wounded. The Canterbury battalion had two companies ashore by 12.30pm, both from the *Lutzow*. They had 45 killed.

Because of heavy Turkish fire, New Zealand troops were not landed between 12.30pm and 5pm at which time the Otago battalion came ashore with the remaining two Canterbury companies. The Otagos had five killed.

The Wellington battalion landed throughout the evening and had one killed. The NZ Engineers and Army Service each had one man killed — a total of 153 for the day.

Later, Spencer pieced together the day's events.

The fight on the day of the landing amounted to this.

The Turkish commander at that point was the famous Mustafa Kemal[1]. [Commander 19th Division] He had a battalion spread out in the positions where we had found them.

All his men had for weeks been practicing [sic] over the ground and knew every inch of it. As bad luck would have it, from our viewpoint, he had two battalions on parade some little distance back, before daybreak, who were about to do a field day on what was to be the battleground.

At this moment reports came of troops landing, not only in his sector, but at other points on the coast which were duly repeated to General Liman von Sanders, the German commander in chief.

Kemal said he was going to move against the Australians at once. Von Sanders told him to wait as he believed our landing was only a feint, that he expected the real and main attack to

Private Martin

Private Meekan

Private Onion

---

1  Mustafa Kemal later became first President of Turkey; granted the name 'Ataturk' — 'Father of the Turks' in 1934.

Private Paine

Private Talbot

Private Thoresen

come up at the Bulair lines where ships could be seen approaching the shore.

Presently Mustafa Kemal got reports that Australians were moving towards Hill 971. He then said, "If that is so, then this is a real attack and I am going forward."

He put the two battalions in motion and rode up to see for himself. His troops and the Australians first collided about 9am as we heard from the ships. Mustafa came up to the next ridge but one from where we were later in action with him, made his reconnaissance, went back to his headquarters to order all available troops into action and to divert other forces, and then moved his headquarters to the ridge he had reached in the morning and there remained for the rest of the campaign.

The comparatively flat ridge over which we advanced was afterwards known as Russell's Top, the track round the head of the gully to our left front became the Neck [sic][1] and the hillside facing us and overlooking us, the Checkerboard.[2]

The Turks had a trench across the gully on our right parallel with our line of advance which accounts for the heavy death roll there so early.

Our men remained in position from the time I was shot, enduring casualties. The sniper who shot Cowdray

1 The Nek, a Turkish position.

2 Better known as The Chessboard, also a Turkish position.

and me was seen by young West from Cambridge who had come up from the rear with number thirteen platoon and was on that flank. West fired at him but missed. The sniper saw West and fired back, also missing. Each fired again and missed.

The Turk firing quickly missed a third time. West cool as a farm boy can be, took deliberate aim and shot his man dead. Laughing with the joy of victory he stood up to look at his late opponent and was hit in the head and killed instantly.

Private Turner

So died gloriously one whom we looked upon as a typical country lad of the true English type despite the fact he was colonial born, stolid in the face of danger and hardship, deliberate, brave and faithful unto death.

Private Boyce

As soon as they had reached the position we had left him in when we advanced, Alderman advanced with the rest of our company and the Canterbury platoons.

Of the latter, John Hill was wounded in the face, the bullet shattering his jaw, and Cliff Barclay and the other subaltern Harry Ffitch killed.

They lay taking punishment until Alderman announced he was going to order a charge. No one knew what he was trying to do but the situation was so puzzling at that stage to anyone who, like most of us, had never been under fire before, that no doubt he felt they could not lie there doing nothing.

Everyone fixed bayonets and rushed forward cheering till the thing fizzled out because of casualties. This business had carried them further forward on the seaward side where they came under heavy fire when Mustafa's counter attack developed, and Baddeley and many others were killed.

It was the head of this attack obviously that we stopped between 2pm and 3pm but the full force of it developed about 4pm and gained some ground until it was finally stopped on Russell's Top. A hundred yards or so further and they would have overlooked the beach.

It was only the presence of the remains of Australians and our men that I have described, that saved the army there from a horrible disaster. Our men fought it out or died on their rifles. No prisoners were taken. I believe the Turks did not capture half a dozen New Zealanders in the whole campaign.

Spencer would discuss the day's events with Alderman and both agreed they had done their best with limited information.

"We could not see there was much we could have done differently with the information and orders that we had."

By day's end, Anzac casualties were around 2000, one in eight who landed. Twenty five are known to have been captured, one of them from Spencer's own company. He was 12/705 Private Thomas Hayes Burgess, died of wounds, September 15, 1915, in Gulhane Hospital, Constantinople. The Turks' casualties were even worse, half their force, 2500 men, were either killed or wounded. Some sources state the Anzacs had 3000 casualties; the Turks 4000.

The Anzacs failed in their chief task — taking Hill 971. Their force which had grown to 16,000, was held, and then nearly driven off by 5000 Turks.

The Anzac landing had been too much a disorganised muddle while the Turks held all the advantages of local knowledge; they held the critically important heights; they had deadly on the ground artillery support and they could quickly deploy their forces once the battle intensified.

Two of the more than 90 pages from the New Zealand Roll of Honour published in Auckland at the end of the Gallipoli campaign.

In the landing at Y beach nearly 3000 British troops landed opposed by a small force of Turks. Instead of advancing, they stopped, awaited orders and an opportunity was lost. The village of Krithia, which the Allies would later have as their main objective in three battles, was deserted. The British troops, Scottish Borderers and Royal Marines, could have strolled in. During the afternoon they faced a counter-attack and were taken out the next day.

At X beach and S beach troops went ashore and faced little opposition. But Y, X and S beaches were the lesser landing points. The main Cape Helles landings were at V beach and W beach and here the British came close to disaster.

After a one hour naval bombardment at V beach — the most important landing point — six steamboats each towing five open boats packed with Dublin Fusiliers approached the shore. At the same time the *River Clyde* drew into the shallows. The Turks held their fire but as the first small boat landed at 6.22am, they opened up with machine guns. The Dublin Fusiliers were massacred as were hundreds of Munster Fusiliers and 2nd Hampshires coming off the *River Clyde*. Some troops managed to get ashore but no progress was made.

At W beach about 90 Turks survived the naval bombardment. They waited also until boats carrying the Lancashire Fusiliers were near the shore and then their machine guns ran hot decimating the hapless Lancashires who suffered 533 casualties out of 950 men. In spite of the small Turk numbers the beach was heavily defended with masses of barbed wire down to the water's edge and artillery and machine gun enfilade fire. Eventually the resistance weakened. Increasing numbers of troops were landed through W beach. By mid-morning some had linked with troops at X beach but were forced back after the Turks counter-attacked.

The French 6th Regiment with two battalions of Senegalese and one of colonial infantry landed at Kum Kale preventing the early transfer of two Turk divisions to Gallipoli. As planned, the French were

## BRILLIANT WORK BY NEW ZEA-LANDERS.

### FIGHTING AT THE DARDANELLES.

#### PER PRESS ASSOCIATION.
Wellington, April 28.

The Government have received advice that the New Zealanders performed brilliant work at the Dardanelles.

The flag at the Post Office was hoisted before 11 a.m. in honor of the occasion.

The High Commissioner in London has received the following message from the Secretary of State:—"His Majesty's Government desire to offer you their warmest congratulations on the splendid gallantry and magnificent achievement of your contingent in the successful progress of the operations at the Dardanelles."

One of the first newspaper headlines of the landing published in New Zealand newspapers. For more than a week details of the landing were sketchy and there were complaints about the lack of information.

taken off next day. The story at Cape Helles on April 25 proved similar to that at Anzac — a smaller force, in this case two Turk battalions, had held off a far larger invasion of 12 Allied battalions. It had been a day of heroism for the Anzacs and Allies but they had not achieved their objectives.

However, the New Zealand and Australian soldiers, in spite of their inexperience and limited training, had shown their exceptional fighting qualities. It had been a concern for the British generals before April 25, 1915; it never would be again.

# Day's aftermath

Having been taken on board the *City of Benares*, Spencer learned the ship could not sail because it had ammunition which was urgently needed for the troops ashore. Eventually, he and over 400 wounded were transferred to another ship, the *Itonis* which sailed for Alexandria over two days after Spencer had suffered his wounds.

During the two day voyage to Alexandria around 14 wounded died and were put over the side.

Arriving in Egypt Spencer was taken to Ras-El-Tin hospital

Fish had accompanied me so far, bringing all my kit and attending to my every want. He was under the impression he ought to remain with me until I got well and my troubles were over. He came to see me about tea time saying , "I went to ask the matron if I should take up my quarters in the hospital; but she fair bit my head off. I'll have to leave you sir. I am going back to the ship." One more parting for me and a sad one. He told us, long afterwards, that he got drunk that night. "I felt I had to sir, before I went aboard. I never felt so lonely and miserable as I did then." He was usually a very sober man. Soon after he was winning good opinions as a sniper on Gallipoli.

Fish was considered one of the best New Zealand snipers on Gallipoli. He was made sergeant of the snipers and personal scout to Captain

J.A.Wallingford although later, for some reason, he went back to being a private. Spencer:

> I gave him some money and got him to send my father a telegram saying. "Wounded. Doing well. Spencer." This he put in at the GPO Alexandria. It arrived before the first list of casualties began to be issued and naturally caused an upset, my father took it into my mother, I was told, saying, "I don't understand this," and then the two old dears burst into tears.

Spencer's telegram reached his parents in Timaru on Monday, May 3. News of the landing had been slow in reaching New Zealand. On Thursday April 29, newspapers had reported the New Zealanders were in the firing line and had done "brilliant work." Next day the Governor, Lord Liverpool, received a telegram from King George V which stated: "I heartily congratulate you upon the splendid conduct and bravery displayed by the New Zealand troop at the Dardanelles, who have indeed proved themselves worthy sons of Empire."

A crowd of nearly 5000 cheered after Liverpool read the telegram in parliament grounds. On Monday May 3, the day Spencer's parents received the telegram Private Fish had sent, there was a hint in the papers of what was to come. "The casualties in the army are necessarily heavy," said the *Oamaru Mail*. Next day the authorities released the first casualty list. Only ten were listed as dead and 119 wounded.

At the same time there was praise. Under a headline, 'The Brilliant Australasians', a Colonel Maude in the London *Evening Standard* said the Australians and New Zealanders were "singularly brilliant in their conduct at the Dardanelles and this will probably exercise a great influence on the German general staff, who formed a very low estimation of their fighting value."

The first detailed report of the landing, written by Ellis Ashmead-Bartlett of the London *Daily Telegraph*, appeared in New Zealand newspapers on Saturday, May 8. A flamboyant character Ashmead-Bartlett had been appointed by the Newspapers Proprietors

Association as special correspondent with the Royal Navy. Charles Bean, the Australian correspondent, said Ashmead-Bartlett was a lover of truth although prone to exaggeration.

"There has been no finer feat in this war than the sudden landing in the dark and storming the heights, above all, holding on whilst reinforcements were landing," Ashmead-Bartlett said. "The raw colonial troops in these desperate hours proved worthy to fight side by side with the heroes of Mons, the Aisne, Ypres and Neuve Chapelle."

Ashmead-Bartlett's dramatic report and the power of Fleet Street helped mould the start of the Anzac legend which rapidly grew. However, if it was not for the intervention of a naval censor New Zealand might have missed out entirely. Ashmead-Bartlett's initial dispatch mentioned only the Australians — the censor added New Zealand forces where required before the final report was published in the newspapers.

Two days after Ashmead-Bartlett's report appeared, New Zealanders read how Lloyd George, destined to be British Prime Minister the next year, told the House of Commons he regarded the success of the Dardanelles to be one of the finest feats of arms in history.

At the time the New Zealand, Australians and other Allied forces had been hammered and were hanging on by their finger nails.

The British press continued to praise the Anzacs.

The London *Evening News:* "The people of Australasia will be wild with enthusiasm for the gallantry of their sons at the front."

*The Star* of London said the story of the Australian and New Zealanders' gallantry stirred their blood. "The young lions of the Southern Cross have come to the aid of the old lion, who is watching their deeds with pride and faith."

And that same day the *Evening Standard* remarked: "The extraordinary difficulties of the landing are overshadowed by the Australasian troops' dash and determination. They suffered severely but it is doubtful whether any other troops in the world would have carried through successfully such entirely individual operations."

The outburst of pride and delight passed as news came of the torpedoing of the *Lusitania* off Kinsale, Ireland, in which more than one thousand people perished and then of the death of New Zealand sporting hero, former Wimbledon champion Anthony Wilding in France.

With each passing day the casualty lists from Gallipoli grew longer and the rhetoric from the editorial writers more bombastic:

"We all mourn the sacrifice of so many intrepid fellow colonists," said the *Oamaru Mail*. "Though such losses are appalling — and all the more so because they are wholly unnecessary — yet those who have fallen went voluntarily with their eyes open, into the jaws of death

Another romanticised view of the landing.

so that they might do their duty to themselves and their fellows.... This war is not to be won by singing 'Rule Britannia' and the 'British Grenadiers.' It is going to rage until one side or the other is exhausted. Britain cannot afford to wait any longer for fortuitous circumstance, but must defend her own strong arm to do her share in subduing the enemy. That her arm is strong is evident by the indomitable conduct of the Australians and New Zealanders in Turkey. The smooth faced boy behind the counter, or from the counting house or factory, or farm, has developed a fighting faculty which transcends all our imaginings. He is no milk sop. If there is a scrap, he wants to be in it, regardless of life or limb. He would rather die a hero than live a coward.....The stay-at-homes might live their hum drum lives till the end of time and not experience a single moment of the exhilaration and the transcendental satisfaction which these heroes won against the oppressor of their country, the assassin of the innocent and the violator of virtue. It is better to have died in such a cause than to live and yet be dead to the spirit which inspired the intrepid souls who did their duty without any thought of the consequences to themselves. Wake up young North Otago! Swarm to the colors [sic], and bring the war to an end." (May 6 and 22, 1915)

# Struggle to live

While the Gallipoli campaign raged on and newspapers in New Zealand demanded more young men volunteer, Spencer endured a desperate fight to live. His right arm was amputated 12 days after being wounded – seven days after he had been admitted to hospital.

When I came to I was at one with Nelson, Raglan, Sam Browne, minus an arm, like many a great hero of the past. I felt as if a load were gone, an icy hand seemed to have been gripping my heart for days and I slept the clock round.

The end of the arm had a bandage on but being so close to the shoulder it frequently slipped off displaying about a quarter of an inch length of blood stained bone, sawn off about two inches below the shoulder. "Why," I asked [Dr] Allen on one of his visits to my bedside "Did you not take it out at the socket?"

"Because we did not want to quite kill you," said he.

"What have you done with the arm?" was my next question.

"It has been disposed of," I was told.

"What a pity" said I, "If possible I would have liked it skinned. The coat of arms of my regiment was tattooed upon it in red and black and I would have liked the skin of that part to cover a notebook with."

Allen laughed. I gathered they were too busy but it would have made a unique notebook cover and I have always regretted it.

Spencer's right knee was also operated on and would remain stiff for the rest of his life. He was soon covered in bed sores and to make matters worse, because the wounds had been neglected so long, he suffered blood poisoning.

At this time he was visited by Captain Price from his battalion, also wounded on April 25, who asked a doctor what Spencer's chances of survival were.

The doctor replied, "I am afraid I cannot hold out much hope."

Those were dark days of which, at times, I must have known very little. I was not at any time worried at the prospect of dying. After all, I reflected, one does not die because one loses an arm. Yet I know the doctors took a grave view as general septicaemia is a serious thing and I was running, I was afterwards told, a record temperature. John Barker of the Canterbury Mounted Rifles visited me and I talked rationally to him and never knew anything about it. Later he was sent for and sat by me for hours awaiting the end. I was quite unaware of all this.

Often-times delirious, Spencer had visions of seeing his dead comrades — Baddeley, Allen, Hobbs, Cowdrey and others.

Night time was the worst of course. In the day time, with the light, there was the come and go to fill the hours and sleep would come in snatches to make up for that lost in darkness. It was in the darkness that the attendants were prepared to hear that I had gone. I would lie there seeing things and when not in pain, had real vision of the world beyond.

A half light would disclose the scene, like the soft

outline of an inspired twilight, a broad still river with trees on the near bank rested the friends of these last days perhaps awaiting the ferry; but any purpose was indefinite.

I knew they were what men called the dead, yet they were living, but these were only a step away awaiting me, and over all was a warm sense of indescribable comfort. With the light the vision faded, but night after night it returned to reassure me, that those I had lost were just across the way.

To join them would mean effortless happiness and rest after a tiresome journey. Amongst those who would gladly have me with them and the group waiting near was not a large one.

For five weeks he remained on the danger list needing morphia for 18 nights to help him sleep. He was terrified that he might become addicted.

Though at first I would not allow myself to take drugs and would not have morphia lest I became an addict, I had to give in as I grew weaker. Once submitting to it, because I could not sleep, morphia grew upon me. I was told I could only have it if I were not asleep at 11pm. Consequently I lay awake counting the minutes to that hour. One night I dropped asleep, awaking to find it was five minutes past the hour, and rang the bell for nurse and morphia syringe.

In came [Nurse] Bodey who said "Ah! Mr Westmacott! You want to sleep. No morphia for you tonight."

It was cruel to taunt me and she made me plead till I got it. There came a night when it was given without demur, but it had no effect, no lovely glow came over me.

At last I called the nurse and said there was something wrong. She evaded direct answer till at last I forced her to admit "Well Mr Westmacott, the medical officer thinks you should give up morphia now, so we have reduced the dose."

After argument I demanded to see [Dr] Cane when he made his rounds later. I asked if I understood the nurse aright. He told me I did. I was very indignant and said "What an outrageous thing. Treating a grown man like a child. If you want me to give up morphia you only have to say so, but this deception is monstrous!"

"You say if we ask you to give it up, you will do so?" he enquired.

"Of course," said I. "You have only to do that. It is reasonable. Deception is not."

"Very well," said he. "We would like you to give it up now. Will you?"

"Certainly I will," I told him, "But now you have tried to deceive me, you must give me a full dose tonight."

"If we do," he laughed. "Will you promise not to ask for any tomorrow night?"

Naturally I will promise anything you ask as long as I am treated properly.

"Give him the morphia nurse," commanded Cane, and sleep soon came to me. It was hard not to ask for it the next night, but I kept my word. This led to a complete confidence in my strength of will on the part of the doctors and the next time I had to go on the operation table which took place five times, and could not sleep thereafter and requested morphia Cane said.

"Are you in pain? If we give it you, will you promise not to ask again unless you are?"

And on my assurance he said, "Give it him sister. He won't ask if he does not need it" and I never again had it more than two consecutive nights.

So life went on till one morning a pleasant faced orderly who had just come on duty, looked at my chart and came smiling to my bedside to say, "Well, you are off the danger list at last sir!"

"Danger list?" I asked. "What do you mean?"

"Oh you have been on the danger list over five weeks," was the reply. "In the morning when we came on duty we used to say 'Well we won't have anything to do for Mr Westmacott today. He was too bad when we finished last night to last till morning.' Now you are going to get well," and I had not known anything about all this!

I looked forward more and more to my afternoon visitors. I had many, generally three or four at least, when fit to see them, as I was now. Wounded officers and men came in numbers, Alderman with his arm in a sling came regularly, Wallingford, [Captain Jesse Wallingford, Auckland Infantry] Hardham VC, [Captain William Hardham VC, Wellington Mounteds, awarded VC in South Africa] on short leave from the front, Ken Gresson shockingly wounded but able to get about now came before his departure by hospital ship for NZ to get messages for my people.

During this time, Spencer was visited by English women. One woman gave him a square watch which he wore for the rest of his life. It had a strap with a clip which he could click on using his teeth and mouth. Engraved on the back were the words;

"The courage that bears and the courage that dares is really one and the same."

The woman who gave him the watch is thought to have been Lady Elsie Carnarvon, wife of the fourth Earl of Carnarvon, and mother of Aubrey Herbert, the interpreter and intelligence officer. She came daily "attending to my every want and filling me with deep religious gratitude," wrote Spencer. "Her faith in God and the blessed hope of salvation in our saviour Jesus Christ was absolute."

Lady Godley, then running her own convalescent home for wounded New Zealand soldiers, visited regularly also.

Nurses and visitors had written letters for him but Spencer realized there were some, personal letters, he had to write himself.

So he began learning to write all over again using his left hand.

After morning dressings he had a nurse prop him up as far as possible and he would start writing. He put in a steady hour day after day. A wounded officer, in civilian life an artist, encouraged Spencer to draw and gave him a sketch book and advice. It was hard work at first but Spencer persevered and even drew a picture from memory of a Sikh sentry at the Suez Canal. The first letter he wrote was to his fiancee in Auckland, Mary Foster.

Writing was difficult because the pull seemed to be from right to left. It was quite a struggle to make it go right. It was suggested that if I followed my instinct and did it that way what I wrote could be read easily in a looking glass. I preferred to force myself to do it right, even though it took longer and [now] I write much better with my left hand than I used with my right. But it took a long time. My first letter, an awful scrawl, was to MF. I told her what a hopeless hash I had made of my life and what a burden I feared I would be from now on to anyone who took an interest in me. It seemed marriage was going to be impossible. I had really had no right to consider it with nothing to offer in the first place, but she must now try to forget me. The letter was posted.

As I lay thinking it over, I had no sense of feeling I had done a good thing, though my reason told me I had done a right thing. It worried me so much that I felt I had been brutal and that what I had written might hurt too much. After twenty four hours I had weakened so much that I wrote again saying that whilst my first letter expressed the only common sense and right course to take, if she still wished to go on, I did also.

Later she wrote to me telling me that the first letter was not what she expected of me but that the second had put things right again. We were as we had always been before the day that I was wounded.

Mary's sister Esther was engaged to Spencer's cousin Rupert, the former officer on *HMS New Zealand* now Lieutenant Rupert Westmacott who had since lost his leg after a raid on Turkish trenches during May. Rupert had given Spencer the Zeiss binoculars he was looking through when first wounded.

> She and her sister Esther were now engaged to two hopeless detrimentals, I with an arm gone and impaired leg, Rupert with a leg taken off. I can understand their father saying he could permit no such engagements. At the same time what he said made no difference to his daughter's decisions, whatever and the question of ways and means was a secondary one. It was apparent EM would be horrified if it were suggested she was dropping a man because he was wounded and maimed for life and in fact she expressed pride in it. Esther never dreamed of such a thing. She was the type to remain faithful unto death. From then on I felt humbled at the idea of such self sacrifice and wrote constantly.

After over three harrowing months, doctors decided Spencer would be taken to England. He received the news that he would go on the hospital ship *Asturias* the next day. That afternoon a colonel visited and Spencer asked what had happened to Allen's and Baddeley's swords. He was told they had been sent to their families in New Zealand. The colonel brought what he said was Spencer's sword to take with him to England.

"He drew from the brown paper a lovely sword. One glance and I felt dashed. I knew at once it was not mine. For my scabbard had a patch on it."

Spencer said nothing and took the sword anyway.

He had made known to Lady Carnarvon he wanted a book of poetry and slept that night not knowing that she left to scour Alexandria on this quest — the only one she came across was an English poetry book for secondary schools. He woke to find it beside his bed.

Taken on board ship later that morning he saw for the first time a newspaper with the casualties from recent fighting at Gallipoli.

Colonel Bauchop

I seemed to have lost every friend who had survived till then. Malone of 1st Wellington, greatest of NZ colonels was killed. Colonel Bauchop, Galahad of NZ officers, was mortally wounded and the list seemed to have no end. Bruce Hay, his adjutant was killed too. [Lt-Col Arthur Bauchop, commanding officer Otago Mounteds; Captain Bruce Hay] The juniors were most frequent. Even poor old Bartrop was dead [Trooper Ludlow Bartop, 41, Auckland Mounteds] but this I got privately. As I lay there, I thought of them and that on this earth we would never see each other again. But I was comforted by what had been revealed to me so recently and told myself. "They have not gone far. They are only just across the way."

Sailing to England the ship called at Malta and then made for Southampton. Arriving in England was the realisation of a dream. He had heard his father talking of his uncles and aunts and it was like coming to the promised land. To them, he was a hero.

We were carried in our stretchers after lunch into a hospital train awaiting us at the [Southampton] wharf on a lovely sunny afternoon at the end of August. I begged to be allowed to sit and see all I could of old England, and the hospital orderlies in the carriage propped me up. Two girls with fresh pink English complexions came through with trays slung in front of them, carrying cigarettes, packets of which they now gave to those who wanted them. The carriage had stretchers along each side level with the windows. It was the first unimpeded view I had had since leaving Egypt and I loved it.

Slowly we drew out of the docks. Looking down on Southampton streets, troops were to be seen everywhere. We were told many were embarking presumably for France. As we went still slowly over a crossing, a platoon was halted at the gates while we passed. They were the first in full marching order ready for battle that I had seen since April 25th. They all looked so young, neat and clean, including the subaltern at their head. New army they were, of good physique, medium height and sturdy. Every red smiling face was keen and eager. I felt proud and encouraged. Little did we know that many were to go straight into battle and be thrown away at Loos within a few days.

In the first three weeks of the Battle of Loos, the British had 2013 officers and 48,367 other ranks casualties. A further 800 officers and 15,000 men were killed or missing. The battle had three weeks to go. German losses were half those of the British.

Soon Spencer's train was in the countryside:

The green fields after the sands of Egypt, the richly foliaged trees after the tall scanty palms were a relief to the eyes, and in the distance all along the route on the higher ground were camps without number. It seemed as if all England were under arms. There were nestling villages we had heard about, each with its church tower, and here and there a manor. The work of the land was continuing too. Men and girls were getting in the hay. They paused in their work to look and wave to us and an old man leaned on his pitchfork and removed his hat to the train as it went by. Could anyone ask a more perfect welcome to the land of his fathers?

Spencer Westmacott recovering in England.

As I write I weep, though I did not then, but my tears are those of gratitude to Almighty God that he spared me to live that day.

On arrival in London he was taken to a hospital for officers, Sussex Lodge, owned by a Colonel Hall Walker, later Lord Wavertree and his wife. His ambulance passed through Hyde Park and he caught a glimpse of his great grandfather's statue, Achilles. Still, four months after the landing, he remained gravely ill. At one point he wrote:

"I felt as if I were soon going into the next world and confided in one or two people that, as I could not be put on a ship bound for New Zealand and be committed to the mighty deep, I would like my body buried beside my grandmother's and aunts at Edington."

After reaching this low point Spencer made a determined pledge that he would get better. Immediately his condition improved.

One of his nurses, Nurse Murray (sometimes referred to as MacMurray) noted the change in a note which is in the Westmacott's family possession:

"Mr Westmacott must now go to bed and stop the letter writing for tonight. He is getting on so well he's no longer an invalid but a cheeky forward young man."

Relations, including his general Uncle Dick, former Lancashire Fusilier colonel Uncle Ruscomb, and Uncle Ned, now back in England, visited him as did soldiers from Gallipoli and Lady Carnarvon who had returned from Egypt. He found his relations had a guilty conscience about Gallipoli feeling the New Zealanders and Australians had been thrown away in a desperate venture.

King George V and Queen Mary spoke with him when they visited the hospital and he was taken on drives through London. During one trip he was shocked to see young women drunk and fighting outside a pub surrounded by others equally drunk and was told they were the wives of soldiers who had just been paid separation allowance. "Was this what their husbands were fighting for?" he asked.

# Campaign ends

Back at Gallipoli, meanwhile, personnel changed all the time as men died or were wounded or fell ill. Reinforcements flowed in from New Zealand to replace them. In short time few of the original force which left New Zealand in October 1914, Main Body men as they were called, remained.

The outline of the campaign went as follows: On May 8, Spencer's Auckland battalion and the other NZ Infantry Brigade battalions had been thrown into a disastrous daylight frontal attack at Cape Helles. Charging over a flat stretch of land covered in daisies in an attempt with other Allies troops to take Krithia and a hill Achi Baba they were machine-gunned down. Eight hundred New Zealanders ended up dead, wounded or missing. They and the Allies never got near Krithia or Achi Baba.

Stints at Quinn's Post[1] in June and Courtney's Post[2] during July followed for the Aucklanders. Then after a return to Quinn's the battalion took part in the major August Allied offensive. On August 7, accompanied by two companies of Gurkhas the battalion leapt forward from the Apex and advanced to take Chunuk Bair. It was a repeat of the Daisy Patch at Cape Helles. In a few minutes over 300 were dead, dying or wounded.

This was the Auckland battalion's last major action at Gallipoli. It

---

1 Quinn's Post, a dangerous post; the Turks were less than 20 yards away.

2 Courtney's Post, another frontline post.

was left to the Wellington battalion to take and hold Chunuk Bair before being relieved by British troops. The shattered remains of the Auckland battalion went to Rhododendron Spur until September 8, when they were taken off with the remainder of the NZ Infantry Brigade to recover at Lemnos. On November 8 they returned to Anzac but stayed only for just over a month until the entire Anzac force was evacuated followed by Helles in similar fashion shortly after. When the news reached London, newspapers again singled out the Australians and New Zealanders for special praise trying to draw positives out of what had proven a defeat.

"The Anzacs won immortal fame, fighting like demons against the best defensive troops in the world," said the *Evening News*. "When their ammunition was exhausted they followed up the enemy with stones and fists. During the Suvla Bay landing the Anzacs, in another glorious attack, gained the crest of Sari Bair. It was not their fault that the rest of the attack was a painful setback."

*The Times* added the British 29th Division in their tribute: "The ease with which the withdrawal was effected will bring intense relief. It is a wonderful organising feat, which will be found as extraordinary as the heroic landing. The immortal 29th division, and the glorious Australian and New Zealand corps, share the chief honours of some of the noblest and most tragic pages of the British Empire's history. The Australian and New Zealand courageous dead lie on the abandoned cliffs. Their memory will never fade."

Amidst similar comments some perceptive thinking appeared.

"This ill-starred and ill-considered enterprise was begun as a minor naval operation, and continued as a major military operation," said the *Evening Standard*.

"It has achieved nothing save an epic of fruitless valour. It has wrecked political and military reputations and has ended like all gambles."

So ended the Gallipoli campaign. The victory was Turkey's.

During the eight months of the campaign, Spencer's Auckland battalion had 19 officers and 410 non-commissioned officers and men killed in action or dead from wounds and disease. In total, 2721

New Zealanders died out of 8550 who landed on the peninsula; 4750 were wounded. Australia's death toll was 8,709 (over 19,441 wounded), Great Britain 21,255 (52,230), France 9798 (17,000), India 1358 (3421). Turkey had over 86,000 killed and 164,000 wounded but some estimate its casualty rates were higher

Having experienced action for only one day, Spencer had been spared the frustration of seeing so many die, oftentimes needlessly. In 1916 the British government appointed the Dardanelles Commission to investigate the campaign. The commission report published in 1917 concluded that from the outset the element of surprise had long gone. "The short naval bombardment in November 1914, had given the Turks warning of a possible attack, and the naval operations in February and March of 1915 led naturally to a great strengthening of the Turkish defences."

Thereafter, the risks of failure outweighed the chances of success, said the commission.

Insufficient planning, an erroneous assumption that resistance would be slight and advances rapid; an under-estimation of difficulties; insufficient munitions and artillery; minor frontal attacks made without adequate artillery preparation; delays after the initial landings deciding what to do; generals who lacked energy and decisiveness at Suvla in the August offensive; Hamilton's failure to examine more critically the situation after the landings; all were highlighted in the commission's findings.

Claims that the campaign was justified by neutralising or containing large numbers of Turkish troops who could be deployed elsewhere were rejected. The only advantages, said the commission, were political.

The General Staff's paper prepared eight years before, recommending such an operation not be attempted, was vindicated.

In 1919 an Australian journalist for the Sydney *Sun* interviewed Mustafa Kemal, the famous Turkish 19th Division commander at Anzac, and later founder of the Republic of Turkey. They met in Kemal's luxurious Constantinople apartment conversing in French, drinking coffee and smoking fine cigarettes.

"It was a mistake to make the naval attack first, and then go away and return," said Kemal. "If a landing had been combined with the first naval attack it would have succeeded, and you would have captured Constantinople. However, we got warning and prepared strong defences.

"We knew weeks before that the British intended to make a permanent landing. I thought that a landing at Anzac would be impossible.

"You made a mistake in trying to hold too large an area. If the Australians had occupied a smaller area they would have held it securely, and with less loss. I saw the mistake immediately, and sent my main force round the left, driving in the flank, while a small holding force opposed your centre.

"We had very heavy losses but we almost destroyed the attacking force, and drove it into a tiny arc on the coast, where it was under the protection of warships. It was a very daring adventure, and if more men had been employed at Anzac it would have succeeded. Only the bravest troops could have accomplished what was done. We feared failure for some weeks, but then our confidence became absolute, and after the Suvla landing we always had the best of the position." (*New Zealand Herald*, January 11, 1919).

# 'Fortune spared me'

Spencer's protracted recovery went on. In December 1915 shortly after the New Zealanders and Australians evacuated, or retreated, from Gallipoli, he went to spend Christmas with a wealthy cousin, Eva Luttrell, at her estate Badgworth Court in Somerset .

His sister Erica came from New Zealand to be with him.

In discussing plans Erica gave my father's advice to return to New Zealand as soon as I was well enough to get military employment before the rush started. I was averse to that. If I could ever be a soldier again I only wanted to be with the Army that was fighting the enemy who was not yet beaten by any means. That seemed a ridiculous ambition for me, disabled as I was. The fact is I shrank from returning to New Zealand a broken man.

Spencer would not return to New Zealand a broken man although his relationship with Mary Foster was cooling.

There had been a showdown between MF and her father in which she told him exactly how she felt about me and what she thought of his attitude. I gathered he was very upset and I see his viewpoint perfectly. Neither Rupert nor I had any money, nor expectations. Rupert would in the end have more than I but then he could not use it. After

MF had done with her father, I gathered he would agree to anything so long as she did not spurn him. To have married and taken a fighting chance, win or die, might have been all right for any able bodied soldier, but to get wounded and lose limbs as we had done, complicated matters all reason. So no engagements were announced, nor could we expect it.

During 1916 he continued his recovery in another home at Bourne—mouth. He was still writing to Mary Foster and feeling it would be a relief for her if they went their separate ways.

She would not put an end to things herself since I had been wounded but I felt I had put her in a difficult position by being so. We had not seen each other since September 1914 yet had written regularly. I had nothing to offer. Marriage to me would mean constant study of economy. She was not used to it. I sensed my mother and sister were against the girl. The latter showed me a letter from my mother saying how M had written to her boasting of the letters she got from other "boys in the trenches."

I could never give her the life to keep her happy in the long run. Marriage to me was out of the question. I now faced that fact finally though it is not an easy thing to do at thirty years of age 'I must go on alone and pray for strength to do it.'

Spencer wrote to Mary breaking off their engagement. He never talked to his family of her. Rupert did not marry Esther either. He married Ruth Gorrie and entered the Colonial Service. Later he farmed in Hawkes Bay but went to live in Wales after his wife died, where he remarried.

One Sunday morning Spencer and other recovering officers were surprised to find Winston Churchill and Sir Ernest Cassel, calling at the home. Cassel was a wealthy banker, financial adviser, friend and supporter of Churchill, particularly in the bad times. They had been on a long walk and looked, according to Spencer, like two tramps.

Seen as the instigator of the disastrous Gallipoli campaign, Churchill was then the most hated politician in England. He asked Spencer where he had been wounded. When told Gallipoli he struck up conversation asking Spencer whether he thought there had been any chance of success on April 25.

Certainly I told him. "It was a good gamble and it did come very near winning quite early."

[Churchill] "If you had any more men. Did you think you could have done it? There were two divisions held back in Egypt you know. If they were put in they might have made all the difference."

A vision of youthful Lancashire cotton operatives in khaki came to me. "Do you consider the Lancashire Territorial Division as one of them, sir?" I asked. "They were hardly ready for an exercise of that kind, do you think? Were they?"

That of course was something he knew nothing about. Apparently one division was like another to him. We all agreed after Churchill left, "That is the end of him anyway. There is no place left for him in public life anymore."

Spencer was soon reunited with his batman Private Fish who himself was recovering from wounds. The authorities allowed Fish to act as Spencer's batman until fully fit when he would return to the line.

They stayed with Spencer's relations around England and went to Ireland where Fish blotted his copybook getting drunk one night. On a train from Newbridge to Dublin he was sick out the carriage window. At Badgworth Court, Fish got to know everyone on the estate. He gave brass buttons with New Zealand Southern Cross stars on them to several farmers and helped out with the farm work.

Haymaking was in full swing and for years after he was

talked of and about the huge forkfuls he swung up to his stack, and all the stories about the delights of life on the land and how he worked in New Zealand that he would tell at smoke or snack times when they paused for a spell, a bite of bread and cheese and a draught from the cider can. I am afraid that all over England, NZ soldiers on leave were painting an exaggerated picture of the life they led; but fields are greenest from such a distance and our little country looked very lovely. Certainly Fish allowed it to lose nothing in the telling and he was never to see it again though war looked very distant those lovely summer days in old Somerset.

Spencer was next based at Roehampton in London where he went to be fitted out with an artificial arm. He and Fish parted company at this time. Fish went back to the line in France. He would die of wounds on February 1, 1918, just over four months after marrying an Englishwoman, Eleanor Scott, at Hinton St Mary, Dorset. He is buried in Lijssenthoek Military Cemetery, Poperinge, Belgium.

Once fitted with his arm it was expected Spencer would return to New Zealand but just as he was about to leave the authorities thought he could be of use co-ordinating the recovery and support of disabled New Zealand servicemen scattered in hospitals around Britain. Early in 1917 he joined the New Zealand Expeditionary Force headquarters in London where "he soon came to despise most of the staff who, he thought, had little commitment to front-line duties and much to the safety and comfort of the rear." (From the *Dictionary of NZ Biography*, Roy Grover). He was reunited for a time with Private Ned Cowdrey who had been with him on Gallipoli and whose brother Albert had died next to Spencer on April 25.

Cowdrey had suffered two bullet wounds on Gallipoli, two more after arrival in France and two on the Somme. He was on light duties. Spencer needed a clerk and appointed him.

Spencer's work at New Zealand HQ ended several months later when he was sent to France as adjutant of the 2nd ANZAC training school near Bailleul. On leave he dated several women, one a former actress widowed in the war and a friendship with a young New Zealand nurse blossomed into romance.

Her name was Jean Campbell, the daughter of Patrick Campbell, an old friend of Spencer's father. While in Sussex Lodge, Jean's father had brought her to visit. A grand-daughter of a famous and wealthy pastoralist William 'Ready Money' Robinson of Cheviot Hills in North Canterbury, she would serve as a nurse in France. A younger brother, Ian Campbell, died aged 18 in France serving as a junior officer with the Cameron Highlanders

Spencer recalled Jean was not the least interested in him when she visited Sussex Lodge.

"Her last memory of him was of an awkward lanky shy youth with a pallid countenance and at this time (in Sussex Lodge) he was a ghost to look at."

Spencer stayed several days at the Campbell home in Cheltenham when Jean was working as a nurse in France. Late in 1917, he accompanied the family, Jean included, to lunch at the Berkeley. Jean had since returned to the family home since her father was ill and dying. Not long after while walking in Hyde Park with a friend Spencer met her and her cousin, Enid Bell. They stopped to chat.

"I surprised myself by suggesting to Jean that we meet in the park on some future occasion and she surprised me even more by saying she would."

A week later they did, under the statue produced by Spencer's great grandfather.

28.10.1917: This afternoon, despite the cold which was bitter, Jean Campbell met me under the Achilles statue. She had on a long fur coat and I wore my own infantry overcoat, so we were warm. We were free of notice of anyone interested in our movements and we walked the park right round to the Watts statue and back by the bridge over the Serpentine where we paused to watch the duck[s]. Time passed quickly. We discussed many people we knew. It was 4pm before we realized the time and went to tea at the Carlton [hotel] where we lingered until it was time for me to drive off and catch the train home to Aldershot.

The relationship grew and Spencer's grave concerns over his future disappeared. By this time he had been told by Eva Luttrell that he would be her heir to the Badgworth estate.

Jean was then working as a volunteer in the former women's prison Wormwood Scrubs, stripping down and cleaning airplane engines.

"My father loved the London scene," Spencer's daughter, Yvonne Riddiford, remembered. "He took my mother to the theatres and he could sing all the songs from the shows years later. Coming back from one show in a taxi he popped the question. My mother said yes. He told the driver to keep going round Hyde Park. They went round three times!"

Spencer and Jean were married in St James' Church, Piccadilly, on September 17, 1918.

Two months later the war was over. At the time he married, Spencer had the rank of temporary major and had been mentioned in dispatches and awarded an OBE (Order of the British Empire).

With peace reigning, he was appointed to the War Graves Commission in London and travelled to France accompanying generals driving round the battlefields to such places as Ypres, Arras, Vimy Ridge and the Somme, assessing the location for future war memorials

At Gravenstafel crossroads he ascertained that the bodies of over 600 dead New Zealanders lay between that point and the Bellevue Spur, many of them still unburied and embedded in mud. Of Passchendaele village he wrote: "This miserable heap of unidentifiable ruins did not look worth fighting for. Yet it was a key position."

He visited the scene where Jean's brother Ian had died on May 9, 1915.

"It was sad to find that the bodies had not been buried in many cases but still lay out on the field in the long grass. Of course they were only skeletons, even the colour of the uniforms had faded."

He was shown the remains of Cameron Highlanders, Campbell's unit, identifiable by the colour of the Cameron tartan where it had not faded in the pleats of the kilts. Skulls and bones were scattered around.

At Le Quesnoy, the mayor called on them and made it known that the inhabitants of the little town regarded the New Zealand division as their deliverers after over four years occupation by the Germans.

In 1919 the Westmacotts returned to New Zealand and Christchurch on the troopship *Arawa*. Still not considered well enough to work his King Country land, Spencer attended the Canterbury College School of Art from 1920 to 1925 and worked part-time as secretary of the Christchurch Club. He produced paintings of his war-time experiences and one of his watercolours, depicting the Anzac landing is in the Queen Elizabeth II Army Memorial Museum at Waiouru.

Unlike some fellow officers, Spencer was prepared for peacetime.

It was with a sense of disillusion and often bitterness that they returned to civil life in a community where, if rank were recognised, it was rather resented than otherwise. This I record with no sense of bitterness. I had studied military history too thoroughly not to know that the return to civil life is hard for the average soldier and when I heard young officers in camp after the armistice discussing what would be done for them on returning to New Zealand, I warned them to expect nothing in the way of privileged treatment when they left the Army.

They could not believe this, most of them had won their way through service in the ranks, and in the field, to a position of great importance as they thought, and they could not visualize a condition of society when it would be forgotten. Yet it was.

Fortune spared me the humiliation and hard poverty too that so many of my comrades experienced after the War.

Compared to before the war Spencer was now reasonably well off. He still owned part of the King Country farm and after his father's death in 1926 acquired sole ownership.

There was no need to go farming. He had a good pension and Jean had means. They had three children – Herbert Patrick in 1921, Margaret in 1923 and Yvonne in 1925. Two years later circumstances had changed and it had become imperative that the family move to the King Country farm.

"He had to go back," Mrs Riddiford recalled. "The farm was under a manager and not in good shape. If he didn't go, he would lose grip on things and lose everything. We went up in 1927 and by then he had returned to England. He came back from England and brought two men from Somerset, one a qualified cheese maker as well as a governess for us.

"Our home was built in the wilds. We lived in extreme isolation – no electricity. Originally he was going to make cheese but it foundered. He went over to sheep."

In time the farm thrived and Spencer developed a routine. Each morning before nine he saddled up his horse. Both this and mounting was quite a laborious process, said Mrs Riddiford, and then he would ride off to look over the property.

"We had a lot of Maori staff but he was a very good manager and had a good eye for stock."

He would return to the farmhouse for lunch bringing a pitcher of fresh water. Then after eating he would write for two hours. He still retained his military interests and commanded the Otorohanga branch of the Home Guard in World War Two.

Spencer Westmacott in later life. He related only small pieces of information to his family regarding his ordeal on April 25, 1915.

Mrs Riddiford: "He could be stern. He was a most upright man and had an Old Testament religion. He used to get the family together on a Sunday and read the liturgy and lesson for the day. He was a very strong, a very honest and entertaining man and a fund of historical recall."

There was also, she conceded, a bit of the old English country squire about him too. Rather controversially he kept using his rank in civilian life and was addressed by it where he lived.

"He was inclined to hold the floor. My mother would have to drive the car. She used to just say 'Yes dear', as they drove along. She was a great support to him. She had enjoyed society life in Christchurch and gave it up to go to the King County, though she was happy there."

Herbert Patrick, or Pat as he was called, shared his father's interest in things military and joined the navy.

Mrs Riddiford: "If he wanted to be on the upper deck you had to go to England in those days. There were two ways you could do it — through a public school or through Dartmouth. So off he went at 13 to Dartmouth. We never saw him for ten years. My parents went back to England twice before the war. My brother had a most distinguished war in submarines and was decorated with two MCs and a DSO."

In 1944 Eva Luttrell died and Spencer inherited Badgworth Court and its estate which included farms in Badgworth and Weare parishes and some in Meare and Mendips. He took Jean and the two girls, Margaret and Yvonne, there for three years living in the manor house which was sold in 1949 becoming an old people's home. (Spencer's son would take over ownership of the farms at Badgworth Estate and Rangitoto. After his death they were sold.) Returning to New Zealand Spencer's health started failing. In 1958 he retired to Wellington. He died there two years later.

"To the day he died he had a military upright bearing," Mrs Riddiford remembered. Jean lived for another seven years.

Like many veterans Spencer did not talk to his family much about the war although clearly he felt a need to pass something on as evidenced by his extensive writing. While he was active in the Otororanga Returned Services' Association it did not intrude upon family life and one of the rare occasions when the events of April 25, 1915, came starkly to Mrs Riddiford's attention was at an Agricultural & Pastoral show in Hamilton, when her father introduced her to Sergeant Ward who had saved his life, and reached the rank of captain later in the war.

"I was a very little girl about six or seven. I can't remember a thing. My father said 'this is the man who saved my life'. I imagine he (Ward) was dairying at the time.

"My father talked only little bits about being wounded. Anzac Day was a special day but he did not go broody on it. He had no time to do that. He was always on the go with the property and other things."

Spencer Westmacott knew that thanks to the bravery of men like Sergeant Ward, and the extraordinary efforts of doctors, nurses and others, he had been given a second chance at life. He counted his blessings that he survived, came home, raised a family and prospered when so many others died and suffered at Anzac.

"Dad had a sharp scramble up a hillside, he was wounded and those men who saved him did a great effort pulling him out. He was saved so much," said Mrs Riddiford.

"I think so many who went through the whole Gallipoli campaign were mentally scarred. He was mentally strengthened. Not scarred."

# Postscript

With the Ottoman Empire defeated in 1918, the Union and Progress government resigned and a new government signed an armistice with the allies. A military tribunal in Constantinople found the three Turkish war-time leaders Enver, Talat and Djemal guilty in absentia of being responsible for the massacre of thousands of Armenians. Talat and Djemal were assassinated by Armenian revolutionaries under a covert plan codenamed Operation Nemesis.

Enver was gunned down in what is now Tajikstan by Red Army soldiers while fighting to establish a pan Turkey state.

The Turks kept fighting to hang onto their land as the Allies began partitioning the Ottoman Empire. In 1922 Mustafa Kemal, the Turkish hero of Gallipoli, demanded Britain give up Constantinople peacefully and added, "If not, we will fight for it."

The British government called on the empire once more for help. As in 1914 the New Zealand government put its hand up to go to war. Within nine days of the first pledge of support, 13,621 men around the country volunteered to go to fight the Turks again. It proved unnecessary. An armistice was called, then a treaty — the Treaty of Lausanne — signed and The Turks got Constantinople. By November 1923 Turkey was a republic with Kemal as president.

Under the terms of the treaty the ground on which Spencer and thousands of other Anzacs fought was preserved forever. Turkey conceded that Anzac would remain one vast cemetery in perpetuity. No rent, tax or other imposition could be placed on it. Access would be free at all times to representatives of the Allied governments and visitors. Anzac so became, and remains, sacred soil.

In New Zealand, Anzac Day was first observed on April 25, 1916. In 1920, an act was passed marking it as a public holiday; this was later amended to ensure the day was observed as a Sunday. Up until 1967 April 25 was one long solemn day with no sports being played, no hotels or shops were open.

Times changed. The Returned Services' Association sensed the mood of the country and from 1967 hotels and eventually shops could open from noon onwards. In recent years Anzac Day has become a greatly important day in the national calendar.

It is a day to remember the horror and sacrifice of war — and to take pride in being a New Zealander.

# Select bibliography

*Anzac: A retrospect*, Cecil Malthus (Reed, 1965, 2002)

*Bloody Gallipoli, The New Zealanders' Story*, Richard Stowers (Bateman 2005)

*Bowler of Gallipoli*, Frank Glen (Australian military history publications, 2004)

*Gallipoli*, Les Carlyon (Macmillan 2001)

*Gallipoli: The front line experience*, Tolga Ornek and Feza Toker (Currency Press 2006)

*Gallipoli: The New Zealand Story*, Christopher Pugsley (Hodder and Stoughton 1984)

*Gallipoli: The Turkish story*, Kevin Fewster, Vecihi Basarin, Hatice Hurmuz Basarin (Allen & Unwin 2003)

*Soldier's life: General Sir Ian Hamilton 1853–1947*, John Lee (Macmillan 2000)

*The Spirit of Anzac: The birth of the Anzac legend*, Patrick Lindsay (Hardie Grant Books 2006)

*25 April 1915: The day the Anzac legend was born*, David W. Cameron (Allen & Unwin 2007)

Various issues of the Gallipolian magazine, Auckland Cenotaph Database and Archway (Archive NZ)

# Acknowledgements

Thank you to the daughters of Spencer Westmacott, Yvonne Riddford and Margaret Wigley, for assisting me on this project, allowing access to their father's writing and providing photographs. Spencer Westmacott's writing is kept at the Alexander Turnbull Library, Wellington. Thank you also to Graeme Leather for book design and Colin Tobin for editorial advice.